MRS. HEERS,

I HOPE YOU — ARE DOING WELL IN YOUR NEW WAY OF LIFE! MY NEIGHBOR MR. BILL & ONE OF HIS FREINDS PUT THIS TOGETHER. I KNOW YOU LOVE

Round About Greenville
AND THE CAROLINA
BLUE RIDGE

YOUR GARDENS, THIS IS SOME OF GODS WORK AT ITS BEST. YOU & FATHER GREGORY ARE A VITAL PART OF MY LIFE, I HAVE ALWAYS ENJOYED OUR CONVERSATIONS, ENJOY THOSE GRANDKIDS!

Love,

Round About Greenville

AND THE CAROLINA BLUE RIDGE

Essays by Pam Burgess Shucker

Photography by Bill Robertson

Copyright © 2020 by Pam Burgess Shucker & Bill Robertson
Essays © Pam Burgess Shucker
Photographs © Bill Robertson

All rights reserved. This book or any portion thereof may not be reproduced or used in any manner whatsoever without the express written permission of the publisher except for the use of brief quotations in a book review.

To purchase books,
email Pam (pamshucker@gmail.com) or Bill (brphoto@bellsouth.net),
or visit local bookstores.
To see additional photographs by Bill: www.brphoto.net.

Published by Pam Burgess Shucker and Bill Robertson,
Greenville, South Carolina

Printed in China through Four Colour Print Group, Louisville, Kentucky

ISBN: 978-0-578-50348-6

Cover photograph: The Middle Saluda River @ Jones Gap State Park.

Frontispiece photograph: Oconee bell, *Shortia galacifolia*, on the Oconee Bell Trail at Devils Fork State Park on Lake Jocassee.

Book and cover design by Janie Marlow, webmaster@namethatplant.net

Preface

Uniquely meditative spots abound 'round about Greenville in South Carolina's natural environment. After hiking thousands of miles through the Carolina Blue Ridge, nature photographer Bill Robertson and I combined our visions and voices into this book, a colorful tapestry of reflections.

Both native Greenvillians, Bill and I have witnessed the amazing transformation of our small Southern town; it emerged from its 1960s identity as the "Textile Center of the World" to become the fourth fastest growing city in the United States in 2018. Periodicals headline it as the liveliest destination in multiple categories. These stories designate numerous exciting adventures to keep a person entertained and stimulated. Few, however, mention the quieter, serene spots that the native knows, places which invite visitors to slow their pace, pause, become aware, and reflect on nature's marvelous gifts.

The tranquil, more secluded locales in the Greenville region shyly extend their welcome also. In this book, we have interwoven descriptions of these relaxing and restorative sites through the photos and essays they inspired. Lists of many of the area's natural highlights, along with addresses and a map, are included in the Appendix.

On excursions through peaceful groves of hardwoods, streams gurgling beside us, and trails winding among spring flowers, Bill and I realize a sense of peace. We blend in this book our artistic expressions and personal experiences to share with our readers some of our favorite places for tranquil retreat and reflection "Round About Greenville."

Pamela Burgess Shucker

Table of Contents

Introduction 10
Thank You, Aunt Margie 17
    Cleveland Park 16
Silent Space 18
    Pretty Place 19
Our Color Saturated World 20
    Rock Quarry Gardens 22
Creation's Interconnections 23
    Lake Conestee Nature Park .25
Beyond Human Senses 27
    Kilgore-Lewis House and Gardens 26
Connections 29
    Prisma Health Swamp Rabbit Trail 28
One-Armed Digger 30
    Furman University 32
Snake Handler 33
    Paris Mountain State Park 33
Community in a Sunflower 34
    McKinney Chapel 35
    Springwood Cemetery 35
    Greenville Churches 35

An oak near Caesars Head shows autumn color.

Feathery Ferns 37
    South Carolina Botanical Gardens 37

Expanding Universe 38
    Poinsett Bridge Heritage Preserve 38

The Holy in Three Deer 41
    Jocassee Gorges 43
    Devils Fork State Park. 43

Black Bear Cub. 45
    Lake Keowee, Keowee-Toxaway State Park. 44

Ancient Sentinel, Earth's Gift. 46
    DuPont State Recreational Forest 46

Decomposition: Nature's Intention 48
    Cades Cove. 49

Blue Ridge Escarpment 50
    Waterfalls 52

Wildflowers!. 56

Flowering Trillium. 60
    Oconee Station State Historic Site, Station Cove Falls,
    Oconee State Park. 61

Tulips and Tigers 62
    Table Rock State Park. 63
    Caesars Head State Park. 64

Water Music. 65
    Jones Gap State Park. 68

Emptiness. 70
    YMCA Camp Greenville 71

Heritage Preserves..................................72
Farm Tools......................................75
   Pisgah National Forest......................75
Uncle John's Country Store......................76
   Campbell Covered Bridge....................77
Tender Accountant Hands........................78
   Hagood Mill Historic Site & Folklife Center...........79
Expanding Circles................................80
   South Carolina Lakes.......................81
Sacred Encounters................................83
   Foothills Trail............................85
Smoky Mountains National Park...................86
Color Spectrum..................................88
   Blue Ridge Parkway.......................90

Acknowledgements...............................93

Appendix 1.....................................94
Appendix 2.....................................97
Regional Map...................................100

THOUGHTS

DISCOVERIES

IMAGES

Introduction . . .

Greenville, South Carolina, sits at the base of the Southern Blue Ridge in a region known as the Carolina Piedmont (the foot of the mountains). In the Southern Blue Ridge Escarpment, the mountains drop sharply — as much as 2,000 vertical feet — into the rolling hills. The landform's dramatic transition creates majestic, accessible viewpoints and waterfalls. Year-round mild climate and beautifully cupping mountains offer a wealth of outdoor adventures.

Greenville's Reedy River Falls descends in cascades from as high as 40 feet. It is one of the nation's few natural downtown waterfalls. Richard Pearis, Greenville's original resident, recognized its power and built his grist mill on the Reedy's banks around 1754; through the years numerous other mills followed, building on land that once served as Cherokee Native American hunting grounds.

In the early 21st century, Greenville citizens realized Reedy River Falls as a unique natural resource and removed the automobile bridge hiding their waterfall from view. Now magnificent suspension Liberty Bridge hangs high above the distinct landscape. It offers pedestrian crossing with incredible views of this once veiled natural beauty. Falls Park on the Reedy surrounds the falls and further unfurls its sumptuous expanse.

Numerous parks offer natural and beautifully contemplative nooks along the Reedy River's banks. The walking and biking Prisma Swamp Rabbit Trail, formerly a railroad line delivering Greenville passengers to mountain locations, now provides a 22-mile car-free path. Plans have been announced to extend these trail connections further through the county.

The mountains call from Greenville! Greenville boasts its own mountain, Paris Mountain, a *monadnock*, an isolated small mountain that rises abruptly from a more gently sloping landscape. Higher mountains create a backdrop for Main Street buildings and roadways. The Cherokee Foothills National Scenic Byway, SC 11, traverses the top of South Carolina, following a former Native American path, and offers serene vistas along the way.

The Jocassee Gorges, billed by *National Geographic* as one of "50 of the World's Last Great Places — Destinations of a Lifetime," is a spectacular gem. First explored in the 18th century by botanists André Michaux, William Bartram, and others, it holds unique species diversity in wild,

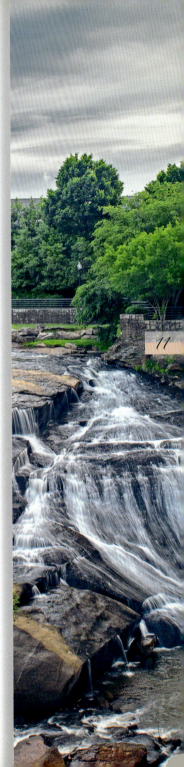

natural beauty. A consortium of organizations in the Carolinas worked for years to preserve this rare area. One hundred fifty thousand acres summon meditators to its natural cathedral, where they are met with rewards such as the ruffled, white spring blooms of the exquisite Oconee bells (*Shortia galacifolia*), endemic to the environs of Lake Jocassee.

State Parks and Heritage Preserves pepper the Upstate, protecting unique landscapes: Jones Gap, part of the Mountain Bridge Wilderness; Table Rock with its iconic view of the legendary table and stool of a great Native American chief; Oconee State Park where the 77-mile Foothills Trail begins; Oconee Station State Historic Site and Station Cove Falls, known for wildflowers; Stumphouse Mountain Heritage Preserve and adjacent Stumphouse Tunnel Park, a failed pre-Civil War attempt to connect South Carolina with Tennessee by rail; Caesars Head State Park, which overlooks the entire region; Devils Fork State Park on Lake Jocassee; Keowee-Toxaway State Park on Lake Keowee; Lake Hartwell and Sadlers Creek State

Reedy River Falls, where Greenville began...

Parks on Lake Hartwell; and many Heritage Preserves. Each conserves a distinctive habitat and offers recreation and retreat in secluded natural environs.

The hectic pace of today's world dominated by doing-acquiring-building-creating-learning-earning-discarding increases the need for quiet pause in beautiful surroundings. Greenville's artful design and extraordinary regional landscape offer tranquil escapes to those who seek them.

Inset: The Gardens at Falls Park on the Reedy River. Initial work to clean up the river area began in the late 1960s, long before Falls Park on the Reedy became a public attraction. The Carolina Foothills Garden Club, with Harriet Wyche as its Parks Committee Chair, worked for several decades to reclaim and beautify areas around the river. Along with this Garden Club, the City of Greenville, Furman University, and other local organizations created today's delightful recreation enhancement of Greenville's birthplace.

At right: Romantic Liberty Bridge at night

15

A space of one breath provides the distance to step back and observe.
— Min-Ken Liao

Greenville's Cleveland Park

At 120 acres, Cleveland Park ranks as the largest park in Greenville County. Much of the park runs as a greenway along Richland Creek and the Reedy River.

Built in 1924 on land given by Greenvillian William Choice Cleveland, through the years the park offered various forms of recreation and quiet, natural space in the heart of town, the types reflecting citizens' interests.

Presently Cleveland Park includes the Greenville Zoo, tennis courts, softball fields, volleyball, the Vietnam Veterans Memorial, eight picnic shelters, the Fernwood Nature Trail, the Ramona Graham Fitness Trail, other wooded trails, and several playgrounds. The Rudolf Anderson Memorial, the Rock Quarry Garden, and a native plant garden also offer quiet retreat.

The Prisma Health Swamp Rabbit Trail runs through Cleveland Park to connect with Cancer Survivors Park, Falls Park on the Reedy, and to link downtown with South Pleasantburg Drive.

Thank You, Aunt Margie

I have often wondered whose early influence stimulated my intense love of the natural world, especially of towering trees and water in all forms. Synchronicity supplied my answer.

My first memory comes before age three when we lived at University Ridge Apartments, built for World War II returning soldiers, and includes meandering creek banks lined with ancient hardwoods. My third birthday celebration at our newly built house involved children sliding down a hill of red clay in the no-grass-yet front yard.

Our apartment consisted of a kitchen so small that without ever taking a step, a cook could fill a pot with water at the sink, put the pot on the stove to boil, while reaching into the refrigerator for fresh greens. The remaining space included a living room with a sofa, an armchair, and a radio on a table; a dining room; one bath; and one bedroom with double bed, dresser, one closet three-feet square, and my sister's crib tucked into a corner. Mother, Dad, and my big sister fit cozily into this small space, until I arrived. Then the delivering doctor asserted, "You need more space."

Behind our apartment flowed five-feet wide Richland Creek, its banks shaded by ancient oaks, hickories, and poplars. The unfenced backyard provided play space naturally accompanied by water music of the creek's flow over rocks and roots. The trees formed a cool, green leaf canopy seeming, to a small child, to stretch all the way to heaven. This natural cathedral more than compensated for the shortage of indoor space, and stretched a small mind beyond cramped gray stone walls into worlds of broadened imagination.

My cousin Charlotte, born my same year, lived across the curve in an apartment like ours. Frequently our mothers exchanged baby-watching favors. One of these exchanges serendipitously provided my first memory, not triggered until decades later by my own daughter.

Our daughter excitedly called to tell us she had chosen an apartment. "It's in a 50-year-old condominium overlooking Cleveland Park."

As I entered the street lined with the canopy of now increasingly ancient hardwoods, the literal roots and water of my birth, a childhood memory flooded me: two small girls, one with golden ringlet curls and the other with a brunette Buster Brown, clasped my Aunt Margie's hands. The two toddled through green grass tickling their short legs. Gnarled oaks and straight smooth gray trunks of yellow poplars shadowed the trek, swaying in the breeze that rippled the ruffles on white pinafores protecting homemade, freshly ironed dresses. The soft music of the small creek trickled through our souls, etching an enduring track on our memories.

Louis Armstrong had not yet sung the song, but my heart unconsciously hummed its words: "I see trees of green…what a wonderful world!"

My first living space may have been tight fitting indoors, but its out-of-doors spaciousness created an enduring desire to be in the natural world.

Both Richland Creek and Reedy River run through Cleveland Park, combining water.

*Silence of the heart is necessary
so you can hear God everywhere —
in the closing of the door,
in the person who needs you,
in the birds that sing, in the flowers,
in the animals.*
— Mother Teresa, *No Greater Love*

Silent Space

"Keep creating space," advises my yoga teacher, advice my body follows as I move deeper into a stretch, my resistive muscles surrendering their daily tension to this gentle expansion. With practice my body becomes supple, more able to respond with less tension and greater grace.

I also need to "keep creating space" in my life, space for silence and solitude; blank white space in which I can read holy direction. Only when we create space for the spiritual will it become alive in us. Spirit is a polite guest who waits to be invited. Creating this emptiness allows us to pause, invite, and wait.

Away from the incessant cacophony of modern living while wandering in the natural world, in the Creator's first revelation, I become aware and discern that quiet voice most clearly. I tread softly under the forest canopy of green shade with fresh breezes caressing my skin, or stride across an autumn field's forever spaciousness, golden grasses waving and birds migrating against azure sky. Some early mornings as the sky turns from inky black to an orange glow, I silently paddle my canoe to the middle of the lake where waves rock me gently, alone in body but not in spirit.

Hiking in the company of friends along a leaf-strewn mountain trail through tangles of fragrant rhododendron and mountain laurel, I also sense intimate spiritual presence. Strolling an East Coast beach's white sandy shores at sunset creates quiet awe as the intense western rays reflect off clouds above and cast pastel hues on approaching aqua waves.

Life will be filled to the last second with minute demands unless we value and create empty spaces to stretch our souls.

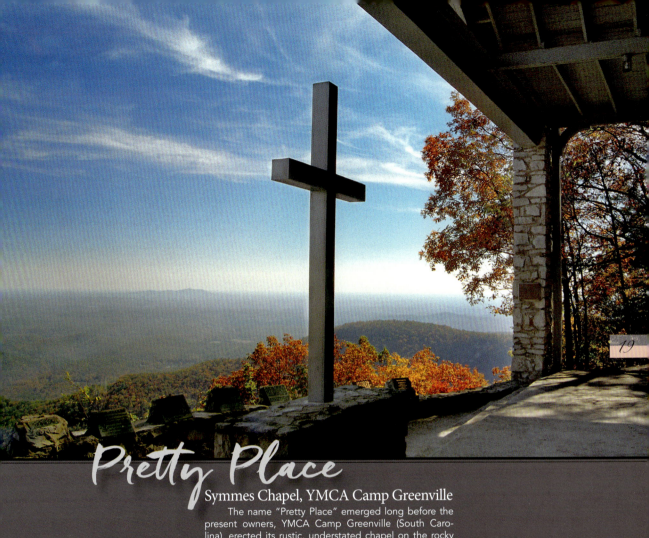

Pretty Place
Symmes Chapel, YMCA Camp Greenville

The name "Pretty Place" emerged long before the present owners, YMCA Camp Greenville (South Carolina), erected its rustic, understated chapel on the rocky precipice overlooking the Jones Gap Valley. Its nickname reflects the essence of this special place. Probably a Cherokee Native American wandering over a century ago along the mountain peak trails of the Blue Ridge front range first gazed out from this spot and uttered in his native language its future name: "Pretty Place!" Millions followed his original gaze with a similar feeling of awe.

The cross at "Pretty Place," Symmes Chapel, visually recreates the intersections at the heart of this book, places to go for reflection, meditation, or rejuvenation in our too busy world. Sacred presence infuses every aspect of creation, "if we have eyes to see and ears to hear."

Our Color Saturated World

Color! This marvelous gift of the natural world rises from our eyes' reaction to light. Imagine our world only in monochrome.

Although black and white photography can reveal spectacularly contrasting images, our soul revels in colors. Most humans choose to surround themselves with color, reflecting individual personality and traits.

Color even influences our senses of taste and smell. The reddest tomato, the most peachy-colored peach, the deepest yellow lemon, the greenest spinach, usually carry the most pleasurable treat for our taste buds, the most intense aroma for our noses, and the greatest concentration of nutrients for our bodies' health. Successful chefs know and practice this secret of nature. As my mother taught me, a colorful plate of food is the most nutritious. (Discounting catsup and mustard!)

21

Often brown indicates death and decay, whereas green means life and growth in our world. My most enduring travel memories reflect nature's rainbow palette: the fiery hues of a Grand Canyon sunset I viewed from an eastern peak; white clouds scattered sparsely in an October sky glimpsed against a backdrop of maples still clad in autumn's finest; a hillside in Switzerland where brown and white cows nibbled green grass interplayed wildly with blue bells, red poppies, and white daisies with sunny yellow centers.

Color gives clues to human health as well. The sick often appear pale, lacking the usual healthy skin undertones. A doctor correctly diagnosed cancer from the paleness of my friend's complexion. Red blood cells whisper "healthy" to the doctor's trained eye. We say metaphorically, "people are blue" when depressed, "angry as fire," or "white as a ghost" when frightened.

Through the miracle of our eyes, color enticingly flows through our world and vocabulary! I gratefully appreciate that our Earth did not burst forth in monotones.

Rock Quarry Gardens
The falls and the present garden were once the site of a pre-Civil War granite quarry, often used presently as a rustic wedding venue.

Above: The Falls at Rock Quarry Gardens in early spring

On previous page: Spring azaleas dominate Rock Quarry Gardens on McDaniel Avenue.

Creation's Interconnections

"Look! See the yellow rectangles?" I quickly zipped the ballooning baggie shut, purposely trapping air. "That's flower pollen the worker bees collected into those pockets on their legs."

Six sets of wide eyes, hued from blue to brown, peered through the clear plastic Ziploc for a closer view of the black and golden insect, confusedly dive-bombing the invisible barrier. During Furman University's summer Scopes Camps, we use hands-on natural experiences as teaching tools.

"The worker bees collect nectar and pollen to feed the larvae that grow from tiny eggs. The queen laid the eggs in the hive cells created by other worker bees."

"Those sunflowers' dark centers guide insects to the flower's pollen. When the insect visits the next sunflower, pollen accidentally scatters onto that flower. That's called *cross-pollination,* and it produces the seed for a new plant. When we eat plants like green broccoli or a yellow banana, we need to thank insects. Without their work, we would have no food."

After opening the zipper and allowing the angrily buzzing bee to fly free, I handed each child a baggie. "Now it's your turn to catch and release."

Two green bins on our porch recycle everything my county collects, and on my kitchen counter a smaller container holds our produce scraps until they are deposited into the big black composter outside. In the magic of that dark, moist environment this plant-based refuse decomposes into nourishing soil supplement, just as nature does with leaves in the forest.

Our home nestles under a tree canopy formed by mature oaks, hickories, poplars, and maples. These deciduous hardwoods provide summer shade, but allow winter sun's warmth through their canopy. They surround our home with a continuously decaying ground cover gratuitously delivered in autumn hues of red, yellow, and orange. A rain garden catches our roof run-off and gradually disperses it through the leafy ground cover to thirsty plantings. We also select our purchases carefully considering true need, no excess packaging, travel expense necessary for its availability, and the way we

Bee collects pollen from a sunflower in Lake Conestee Nature Park.

24

will eventually dispose of the item. When we finish with an item that still has value, we donate it to others. As the billboard for Goodwill reads, "It is all good! Donate."

Government leadership often chooses *economy* over *ecology*. Both words root in the Greek word *ecos*, meaning *home*. Concern for our home's foundation, the limited natural resources of our earth, must take precedence over the decoration of our home.

Earth's ability to continue depends on our decisions to live sustainably, allowing the natural resources we consume to reestablish. "The good life" does not come from buying and accumulating material possessions and wealth.

Revealing the sacred hidden in this natural world continues as my life purpose. With gratitude, I communicate the exquisitely balanced and interconnected creation we are graced to inhabit, but which now teeters perilously from our lack of thinking sustainably.

Lake Conestee Nature Park

This 400-acre natural habitat considered an "Important Bird Area of Global Significance" and a "South Carolina Sanctuary for Wildlife" lies on the Reedy River just six miles from downtown and provides an example of recycling at its best. The Reedy River, where Greenville began, once served as the trash dump for mills and industrial waste. The mills disposed of excess dyes in the river; Lake Conestee and Mill were at the southern end of the line. Conestee dam caught what floated downstream and retained it. Each morning during the 1960s, my family played a game to guess what color the Reedy would be that day!

Labeled toxic, the beautiful forested land lay dormant until the Conestee Foundation proved it could be safely used as a nature park. An extensive trail system offers hiking, biking, and wildlife exploration in its beautiful natural setting. Forests, meadows, lakes, vernal pools, and emergent wetlands offer unique habitats and abundant species diversity. This easily accessed retreat can be enjoyed during daylight hours using maps available online at: www.lakeconesteenaturepark.com.

*To live simply
is to live gently,
keeping in mind always
the needs of the planet,
other creatures, and
the generations to come.
In doing this
we lose nothing,
because the interests
of the whole naturally
include our own.*

— Eknath Easwaran, *Original Goodness: On the Beatitudes of the Sermon on the Mount*

Kilgore-Lewis House and Gardens

The Greenville Council of Garden Clubs moved the local 1838 Classical Revival mansion, listed on the National Historic Register, to its present location to serve as the organization's headquarters.

The extensive gardens surrounding the house overlook a restored spring and placid pond and offer an example of a certified South Carolina Backyard Wildlife Habitat.

The Kilgore-Lewis House sits in one of eight designated Historic Districts in the city, East Park Avenue. Other Historic Districts include: Colonel Elias Earle, Hampton-Pinckney, Heritage, Overbrook, Pettigru, Woodside Cotton Mill Village, and WestEnd. The Village of West Greenville offers the arts district.

> *Not knowing when the Dawn will come, I open every Door.*
> — Emily Dickinson

Beyond Human Senses

Our human senses and intelligence cannot detect whole worlds that exist in our universe. But our souls, our consciousness beyond thinking, can. The Spirit world engulfs us, but most people live every day unaware of this existence. As earlier cultures have known, animals often attune more to these worlds than humans.

Dogs hear sound vibrations that the best human ears do not intercept. I often walk my dog on a street in which other dogs reside inside other homes. Sensing our presence through his many additional receptors, invariably the dog inside the closed house will begin barking as we silently (I thought) approach. For every dog, a walk around the block becomes an olfactory smorgasbord that escapes the most discriminating human nose.

Frequently my canine buddy reads my unspoken thoughts. We usually follow one course on our neighborhood walk, but if I think of turning a different direction, somehow he senses my intentions and walks ahead onto the unusual route.

Light that human eyes cannot distinguish exists at both ends of the light spectrum. Humans can see only the colors termed "the visible light." Birds' eyes detect additional light. Ornithologists have determined that birds exhibit infrared color patches indicating their sex and species to each other, but these differences remain invisible to us. Although to human eyes many birds look identical, these tiny flying feathered balls find the other sex within its own species, and proceed to mate.

Insects also see colors beyond those we see. The varied patches of color on flowers indicate the best source of pollen. No matter what the main color of the blossom, the center where fertilization of the stigma can occur usually differs in color. These pollen guides direct insects to the area of the flower in which the best chance for fertilization can occur. Whether inside the tubular neck of the daylily, tucked into a recessed pocket of the lady's slipper, or peeking out above the white petals of bloodroot, these often-infrared colors signal the most advantageous journey to pollination.

The languages of nature offer apertures to worlds that our five senses cannot take us. Often our busy lives do not leave time to learn. Increasing our awareness and attention to nature's messages can be our tutor for undetected dimensions of our world.

Kilgore-Lewis House and Gardens

Prisma Health Swamp Rabbit Trail

Greenville offers multiple connections through construction of the walking and biking path named the Prisma Health Swamp Rabbit Trail. The former rail line once delivered Greenvillians to northern towns and gathered the nickname as it passed through some boggy terrain along its route. Presently the SRT connects Travelers Rest with downtown Greenville for 22 miles. Future connections will extend the popular trail to many other neighborhoods and areas of the county. While the trail is very heavily used on the weekends, weekdays offer a wooded quiet retreat with many interesting stops along the way. Early mornings may also include encounters with a spider's web across the path!

Connections

I took a lake seat
and watched Earth
glide into orangey glow.
Wrinkled skin contained
forested banks wavering
in mirrored light: water reflecting
light reflecting shore reflecting
light, all, all intertwined
dancers in the dawn.

Tilting skyward, my head
touched and tangled; my hair
netted, entrapped.
Swishing, my hand
stopped, mid-air:
Light, just right, illuminated her
labor, her nightly creation,
preparing her solitary meal.

Surely this must be
the best café in town!
Twenty cups woven
round corners, between
everything upright.
Patient spirals awaiting
night's entree.

But alone she worked.
Alone she wove
her inner resources,
stronger
than steel. Alone
she captured, wound, and
consumed her meal:
each flying, crawling
creature
and her mate.

Dawn now, she begins
devouring her work
line by line.
Her circle of cups unwoven
she retreats to a hidden
hollow, alone,
awaiting night's cover.

A repeating cycle
till her last web
shelters a nest of eggs
and she departs alone
to die.

One-Armed Digger

> If the sight of the blue skies fills you with joy,
> if a blade of grass springing up in the fields has
>   the power to move you,
> if the simple things of nature have a message
>   you understand,
> rejoice, for your soul is alive.
>   — Eleanora Duse

Sometimes I saw him digging as I passed his home on my daily walk to and from school. His right hand clutched the shovel handle tucked into the crook of his right arm as his left sleeve hung empty, swaying in sync with the shovel strokes.

I glimpsed beside him not one bit of green, nothing growing or alive. Only humps and valleys of South Carolina red clay rose and fell, mounds of earth haphazardly interspersed between gullies descending waist deep as he dug. "The crazy one-armed man who dug his yard for treasure," we called him. We passed as swiftly as we could, fearful that he might come after us with the shovel. Confirmed in our minds by the holes we witnessed, the rumor formed that he believed treasure was buried in his yard, so he spent the days of his life digging to discover what he believed to be hidden wealth.

As an elementary school child, whose world opened to new treasures each day, I marveled at the one-armed man excavating his yard, but I never dug deeply enough to discover his true story. Many years later, I pass the

Furman University's venerable Bell Tower, a replica of the original on the downtown campus, reflects in the sunset on the Furman Lake.

31

The entrance gates welcome visitors to the Furman University campus.

location of his home and wonder what became of him. Once precariously balancing among the mounds and holes, his house eventually fell to commercial development; cars now travel past at 45 miles an hour.

Sadness fills me when I think of the one-armed man. While seeking in his red earth holes for buried treasure, he eliminated all possibilities for growth, both his own and the earth's. What a transformation would have greeted us children if he planted as he plowed. Grass greening in springtime with native dogwoods blooming white, or daffodils spreading their sunny yellow glow in the morning light, or crocus peeping through the snow; he missed them all. He only dug and searched, looking down into the clay he mounded each day.

I wonder: Did the sale of his land become the "treasure" he sought or did development arrive after his life hung as empty and limp as the left sleeve where his arm should have been?

Furman University

Recognized as one of the most impressive campuses in the United States, Furman University broke ground at the present site in 1953, just six miles north of downtown. This new campus combined two former schools located in the heart of Greenville: Furman University since 1851 and Greenville Women's College since 1856. Created of Georgian-style red brick architecture with beautiful views of the Blue Ridge Mountains, the campus now sits at the foot of Paris Mountain, on land that had been extensively farmed for cotton. Every tree, shrub, and grass of the gorgeous landscape surrounding its centerpiece, the Furman Lake encircling its iconic Bell Tower, has been planted since the 1950s, amazingly demonstrating how land can be healed and restored. Furman is the oldest private institution of higher education in South Carolina and offers coeducational liberal arts degrees to its 2,700 students.

Snake Handler

I've not always been a snake handler. As a child, my greatest fears, and often my nightmares, centered on snakes.

One summer day when about seven, neighbors invited me to go with their children to Paris Mountain State Park, a nearby mountain park, to pick the lovely purple and lavender violets covering the slopes. After picking a variegated handful, my small fingers reached for a delicate blossom wearing my favorite deep purple. Instead of velvety violet, my hand brushed smooth back scales of a glistening black snake stretched and warming lazily in the morning sun. Screaming hysterically while scattering a trail of purple behind me, I fled up the hill to cower in the car. The neighbor parents tried to reassure me that I had mistaken a stick for a snake, but I would have none of their platitudes. I shook and cried all the way home! My parents downplayed the entire episode, but my fears cemented. Real or imagined, that snake symbolized my feelings towards "slithering, scaly reptiles" throughout my young life.

I began teaching in a magnet school, Roper Mountain Science Center. Naturalist and master teacher Peter Deboer became my mentor. I took in as much new information there as the elementary school students.

Deboer taught first graders classification by observing the material covering animals' bodies. He demonstrated with different live animals, encouraging each child to notice the body covering: mammals' fur; amphibians' smooth, moist skin; birds' feathers; and reptiles' scales. To add a tactile experience to his oral and visual lesson, I held the animals for each child to gently touch "with one finger."

I was fine with each animal — until the snake! I had never

One of the trails at Paris Mountain State Park

Paris Mountain State Park

Once a protected water source for Greenville, Paris Mountain State Park, located five miles from downtown, offers recreation of all levels including quiet paths for hiking, swimming, kayaking, paddle boating, mountain biking, camping, and picnic facilities.

Many buildings originally built by the Civilian Conservation Corps in the 1930s have been preserved and re-purposed; the old bath house now serves as the office, classroom, and ranger station. Hiking trails of all levels pass lakes, streams, and rocky creeks, beginning with circling Lake Placid, the park's centerpiece.

touched a snake and — after my unintended childhood snake encounter — never felt a desire to! As an adult attempting to teach children to be unafraid of reptiles, I had no choice but to cup my hands and drape my forearm with an orange-and-brown-patterned corn snake. Trying to still my racing heart, I gently extended my squirming partner toward eager eyes, which watched and evaluated my reaction. Small fingers lightly stroked the scaly, surprisingly not slimy, skin. Dramatically I turned its underbelly up for each child to discover the black and cream checkerboard pattern on its underside.

During that day's lesson, the children and teacher together overcame centuries of ingrained, irrational fear and gained new respect for one of God's valued creations. Almost reluctantly I returned my new friend to its aquarium.

Community in a Sunflower

Three layers of green bracts, pointed and veined, rise from the firm stem. In the summer's heat these bracts open in a circle of golden flowers mimicking their name, sunflower, a golden symbol of summer's hospitality.

Often mistakenly called petals, sterile ray florets create a yellow community spiraling around another circle of chocolate brown disc florets. Each disc floret maintains the ability to reproduce. When fertilized by pollen transferred on a visiting insect from another sunflower, each disc floret's ovule can mature and become a seed. By summer's end, the spiral center contains hundreds of seeds, future sunflower plants, and food for hungry migrating birds.

Flower composites echo the human need for community. Although each disc floret is a complete flower, the plant constructs a more viable life by living in communion. The ray flowers' yellow catches a flying insect's attention and offers an inviting perch while it sips the blossoms' nectar. As it sips, the visitor leaves behind pollen from another. Each flower can mature and reproduce only through the aid of a pollinator.

I also need community to mature. One of my fondest memories centers on a white clapboard church in rural South Carolina near my father's home. During "July 4th Homecoming" people celebrate *community* found in this sanctuary. My father, his brothers, and our families joined this celebration over several years of my childhood.

Unpainted wooden and often warped picnic tables bowed with the wealth of fragrant homemade dishes. In a metaphoric embrace, ancient oak limbs spread over the community, sheltering participants during this hospitable feast. The church's adjacent cemetery held deceased members' graves, extending these celebrated relationships back five generations.

Sometimes only a simple wooden structure, the church's combined community, like the sunflower's yellow and brown circles, offers a member the chance to flower, produce seeds, and develop individual talents that brighten the world. We humans, like the sunflower, must open to the gifts freely offered by the sun, the insect, and the community. A tightly closed bud never matures nor does a person who attempts to live without relationships.

McKinney Chapel

in Eastatoe Valley was constructed in 1891. A nondenominational service is held there on the fourth Sunday of each month, and its annual old-time Christmas pageant is well known (*above right*).

Springwood Cemetery

(at right) is listed on the National Register of Historic Places as the oldest municipal cemetery in South Carolina. As many as 2,600 of its 7,700 graves lie unmarked and are believed to be those of African-Americans and the indigent.

Greenville Churches

Churches have been a vibrant part of Greenville from the beginning. Early Founding Father Vardry McBee, whose statue stands at the corner of Court and Main, gave downtown land to build churches for four denominations: Christ Church Episcopal, First Baptist, First Presbyterian, and Buncombe Street Methodist. These congregations, three still on major downtown corners, welcome visitors.

First Baptist Greenville moved to 847 Cleveland Street where a beautiful labyrinth beside the front gardens offers a meditative experience to anyone.

Ferns of many types find a haven in moist environs such as the Natural Heritage Trail in the South Carolina Botanical Gardens on the Clemson University campus.

Feathery Ferns

Spring reawakens leisurely. Like feathers, fern fronds silently caress the wind as it stirs fringed edges, and they warm to the filtered sunlight sifting through multi-hued green leaflets. Imitating the tight-coiled end of a violin and thus called a fiddlehead, lacy fern fronds unfurl and stretch toward light. Woodland ferns, like spring ephemerals, must capture the sunrays necessary for growth and reproduction before the forest leaves emerge and shade prevails.

Some of the first plants on earth, ferns are vascular plants, that is, those with supporting tissue needed for life on land and conducting tissue that moves water and nutrients through the plant. They appear in fossil records 350 million years ago. As the dinosaurs roamed in search of food, they treaded on and nibbled ferns. Ferns preceded more advanced flowering plants, which reproduce by creating blossoms that mature into seeds.

As herbaceous plants, ferns lack the woody stems and branches of trees and shrubs and thus grow low on the forest floor. Many ferns have *rhizomes* (underground stems with nodes, buds, and roots), and some use these to reproduce by sending out creeping extensions that create new plants.

Ferns also reproduce by creating *spores* inside of *sporangia*, a more primitive reproductive system than seed-producing flowering plants. Clusters of sporangium, called *sori*, usually appear as brown dots on the underside of the frond's leaflets, or *pinnae*. When ripe, the sporangia open to release the spores. The spores are broadcast by wind, water, or even animals.

The reproductive cycle requires moisture for transfer of the sperm, thus ferns in the Southeast often live in damp, shady environments. Decomposed leaf and downed wood litter from previous years create the topsoil of the forest floor. The decaying wood produces a moist, rich environment in which many ferns thrive and which enables prolific reproduction.

Those who study ferns in their natural habitat are called pteridologists and ferns are scientifically classified as Pteridophytes. Whether we consider ourselves a pteridologist or not, the forest is much more lovely when enhanced by ferns.

South Carolina Botanical Gardens

The South Carolina Botanical Gardens, located on the Clemson University campus, include nature trails, ponds, pathways, streams, woodlands, and a meadow. Included in the garden proper are the Hanover House, an early 18th-century house constructed in the South Carolina low country; a pioneer village featuring the Hunt Log Cabin built about 1825; the Bob Campbell Geology Museum; and the Natural Heritage Trail, which incorporates native plants from every region of South Carolina: the mountains, the upstate through the midlands to the low country, all viewed in one short walk. In 2017, Patrick McMillan, Hilliard Professor of Environmental Sustainability and Director of the South Carolina Botanical Gardens, identified three ferns unknown before to grow in South Carolina, found within the extraordinary diversity of the nearby Jocassee Gorges.

Poinsett Bridge Heritage Preserve rests in winter and spring beauty.

EXPANDING UNIVERSE

The most influential realization of the 20th century may be the continuing expansion of the universe that we call *home*. First proposed by Albert Einstein, physicists now base all theories on this belief known as Hubble's Law. Experiments proved beyond their doubts and theories that indeed the universe constantly moves outward. Most of the rest of us, when we consider it, accept this postulation as fact.

The theory of an expanding universe states all matter, including light and its resulting energy, was once compressed into a composite glob spinning in vast, incomprehensible space. An instigating force caused this ball of matter to explode, in vernacular referred to as "The Big Bang."

The force that instigated the explosion of the mass of matter continues, pushing all components outward from its center. With no opposing force, no gravity resulting from other spinning matter, the broken particles expanded in ever-widening gyres. Eventually the spinning of larger particles created a force that attracted other particles into the pulling gravity of their spin, creating systems revolving in unison with the larger mass.

To me, the instigating force was "God," my naming word for Ultimate Good, the creative force in this universe. This creative spirit for ultimate good created all, and included a spark of that same fire within every particle of matter. All life desires to create, to expand itself outward.

This spirit to create, to expand, is inherent in our universe and the essence of every component of it, from quarks to stars, with us sandwiched between. All conscious life knows it will not last forever; all must die. We humans, and probably many animals, desire to leave a legacy, to make our mark that says, "I lived; I was here."

Intuitively we know we will not live forever, so we create: children, works of art, businesses, and dynasties, networks that we hope will live after us. We expand ourselves in this way, just as every bit of matter in the universe is expanding simultaneously with its own dying. Life begets life, and death.

Poinsett Bridge Heritage Preserve

Poinsett Bridge, built in 1820 from locally quarried stone, served as part of a road from Columbia, South Carolina, to Saluda, North Carolina. It is the oldest bridge in South Carolina and perhaps in the entire southeastern United States. Named for Greenvillian Joel Roberts Poinsett, who served as United States Ambassador to Mexico and for whom the Poinsettia flower is also named, the area is now a South Carolina Heritage Preserve offering hiking and picnicking by a lovely Little Gap Creek.

Remember, we don't inherit the earth from our fathers, we borrow it from our children. And if you borrow something you don't have the capacity of paying back, you are actually stealing.

— David Brower, Backpacker: The Magazine of Wilderness Travel

> There is
> in the depths of every moment
> a gate
> that grants access
> to the depths of God.
>
> — James Finley,
> Center for Action and Contemplation
> Daily Devotions

The Holy in Three Deer

On my walk one October morning, three deer, a doe and two smaller fawns which had already lost their spots, emerged from the field, but hesitated to cross the pavement. They sensed my progression toward them before their movement created my realization of their presence. There they paused, motionless, 75 feet in front of me. I froze. I wanted so much to observe them longer, to not scare them off from their mission of grazing the tender grass on the other side of the road.

The doe's head slightly turned toward me, evaluating my threat to her and her offspring. We stood motionless for many moments. She then began to unhurriedly cross to the freshly cut lawn on the other side, her fawns following her lead. The fawns nibbled as they slowly and silently followed mom from the grassy edge into the higher

Dramatic view from Jumping-Off-Rock showcases Lake Jocassee in the Jocassee Gorges.

brush. All the while I stood on the road, silent and still, but watching intently.

As the brush clouded both their view of me and mine of them, I inched closer. I froze again when my eyes separated them from the forest edge. The three, still wary, waited again, still and silent, but with heads raised alertly. After several minutes of shared motionless but heightened vigilance, mother walked further into the woods out of my sight. The two fawns remained without moving. The slightly larger fawn continued with head turned to gaze my direction. Our eyes met without fear or acknowledgement: mine desiring not to disturb or frighten them; his or hers evaluating the threat I posed, protective of the smaller sibling.

Finally, I felt I needed to release them to eat in peace. I quietly moved into clear view. The larger of the two, silently stamped its foreleg and

Devils Fork State Park, Lake Jocassee

the two turned to wander slowly into the forest grove.

I exulted in this sacred moment of awe. I felt appreciation and respect for one of earth's inhabitants with whom I seldom have the privilege of a close encounter. Indeed, for me, one of life's creations delivered a gateway to the Holy's embrace.

Jocassee Gorges

National Geographic listed Jocassee Gorges as one of "50 of the World's Last Great Places — Destinations of a Lifetime." The Jocassee Gorges, shared by North and South Carolina, ranks as a Globally Biologically Significant Area because of the diversity of species found within it.

Jocassee Gorges is a second-growth forest that recovered during the 20th century from devastating damage by both humans and nature: major flooding after the break of Lake Toxaway Dam and logging by the next owner, Singer Sewing Machine Company. Duke Energy Corporation bought the land in mid-century for hydropower production.

High rainfall in this temperate rainforest (over 80 inches per year) and steep topography proved perfect for development of a pumped storage system. Using three connected lakes, this system captures unused electricity during times of low use and produces power for the area more efficiently. A tour available at **World of Energy** at Oconee Nuclear Station educates on the pumped storage method.

The **Gorges State Park** Visitors Center in Sapphire, North Carolina, received certification as a LEED Building, Leadership in Energy and Environmental Design. A collection of photographs of waterfalls in Jocassee Gorges taken by photographer Bill Robertson hangs in this building.

Devils Fork State Park

The lovely bloom of Oconee bell, *Shortia galacifolia*, magically emerges early each March to carpet the banks of Lake Jocassee.

In 1787, here in the valleys of the Carolina mountains in the now permanently protected Jocassee Gorges, French botanist André Michaux encountered the plant and collected a specimen for the botanical museum in Paris.

Over 50 years later, American botanist Asa Gray saw that specimen, and realizing that it was an undescribed species, named it *Shortia*, for a botanist friend Charles Short, and *galacifolia* because of the leaves' similarity to Galax leaves. For almost 40 years thereafter, Gray searched for the plant in the wild, but *Shortia* was not found again until 1877, by a teenager named George Hyams.

Its delicate bell-shaped flowers and the area where it was first discovered ("Oconee") combine to form its common name, Oconee bell.

Devils Fork State Park offers the Oconee Bell Trail, a mile-long path beginning behind the ranger station and meandering through a forested area and pond, following a stream bank habitat of this serrated-leaf native found in only a few counties of the United States.

Oconee bell, *Shortia galacifolia*, on the Oconee Bell Trail at Devils Fork State Park on Lake Jocassee

Lake Keowee, Keowee-Toxaway State Park

In addition to offering camping and hiking, Keowee-Toxaway State Park houses the South Carolina Information Center for the Jocassee Gorges and a Native American exhibit. Lake Keowee inundated the site of the old Cherokee town of Keowee, meaning "land of mulberry groves." Created by Duke Power for hydroelectric power generation, Lake Keowee, Lake Jocassee, and Bad Creek Reservoir provide a stable water supply and generate power for upstate South Carolina. Lakes Keowee and Jocassee offer many recreation opportunities.

> *The future can exist only when we understand the universe as composed of subjects to be communed with, not as objects to be exploited.*
>
> — Thomas Berry, *The Great Work: Our Way into the Future*

Black Bear Cub

A tiny coal black, furry ball, 30 pounds and stream soaked, bounded up the grassy hillside from the creek bed as I stepped on a dry twig and rustled the greenbrier tangle of end-of-summer undergrowth. My old black lab, busily sniffing in another direction, failed to detect the retreat just 50 yards away. I first thought "dog," but then realized its bounding gait was not that of a dog. The little bear cub fairly bounced along as it ascended through the woods, I suppose to find mama.

Little Cub, did you find mama? Was she close by eating huckleberries, awaiting your return after your stream detour?

I fear she may not have been.

At the top of this hillside, stores line a busy highway, once forested land now clear cut for urban development. Natural forests connect narrow seams of dense vegetation used as wildlife transportation trails. Small pockets like these hardwood coves remain because they are so steeply "veed" that clearing them creates a hazard. Developers often leave these hollows untouched. Pink flags even here may signal their future replacement by development.

Recent news from a coastal golf resort relayed the killing of a "nuisance" male alligator 11 feet long. This creature, the length of two human animals laid feet to head, lived peacefully 60 years or more in this pond, never bothering with any interference bigger than his next meal. Which did not include those he terrified, or those who captured him and decided his demise! The pond, now decreed a golfers' "water trap," could no longer contain any reptile larger than a turtle. So, this living fossil had to be removed from its pond home, which it occupied first.

In some places people peacefully share habitat with wildlife, each allowing the other to live and let live, mutually occupying space and each working to gather what each needs. But that was not to be the fact and fate on this coastal course. Play through continues; gators must go!

Will the black bear cub suffer a similar loss of habitat and life?

*Facing page:
Lake Keowee boasts
300 miles of shoreline.*

Ancient Sentinel, Earth's Gift

Squirrels scold my intrusion as my step crunches dry leaves and a twig snaps. The ancient tree ahead presents a commanding presence, the oldest living creation my leaf-softened footfalls tread near this day, and the toughest. Old, resilient, essential: her cycle of growth and death both create and enable all life forms supported by our earth's delicate balance.

Tree life usually begins as cross-pollination creates a seed that lies dormant until moisture enters its external casing. Initially the endosperm within the casing feeds the emerging embryo until the sprouting stem swells, cracks its outer cover, and breaks into light. The roots descend into dark, moist earth as the stem seeks light. A new tree begins life; and it offers life.

The adult tree grows around the baby sapling, evidenced as the center core in a cross-section, when each spring and summer new cells encircle it. The older dead cells pushed outward thicken into the wizened bark layer, protectively enclosing the darker burnished-red heartwood core with defense against assaulting elements. Growth rings alternating light and dark develop within the trunk. The pattern of rings in a cut or cored tree reveal yearly growth. Dark rings laid during the summer months age the tree and all rings provide clues of surrounding weather conditions.

Above: Lake Julia's decaying log and autumn leaf colors in DuPont State Recreational Forest demonstrate nature recycling itself.

DuPont State Recreational Forest

Scenes shot here for the movies "The Last of the Mohicans" and "The Hunger Games" reveal the beauty of the 10,473 acres filled with waterfalls, rivers, and forests.

Citizens who recognized its unique diversity and natural recreational opportunities petitioned North Carolina and saved Dupont from becoming a gated community.

Internal heartwood layers, although dead, remain steel-strong through lignin gluing together cellulose fibers. Surrounding heartwood is sapwood, or *xylem*. Young xylem moves water and minerals from roots to leaves; as xylem ages and dies, it becomes more heartwood. Between sapwood and bark lies *cambium*, a thin layer of growing cells which may become xylem or *phloem* (inner bark). Phloem transports sugar and nutrients from leaves to the rest of the tree.

Using a green pigment called chlorophyll, leaves convert sunlight into sugar. While performing this function, leaves also absorb carbon dioxide from the atmosphere and expel oxygen as a waste product, which nourishes other life forms. *Photosynthesis* remains one of the miracles that allows life to exist on this planet.

Environmental assaults destroy natural bark protection and create openings for deterioration. Damaged, these defenses begin a slow decline to decay and death. Eventually the tree's formerly healthy cells decompose, releasing nutrients to nourish new life.

In nature's delicate balance all life ends in decay: decomposed cells recycle into nourishment for future growth. Ancient civilizations knew and honored this most basic principal of earth. Just as nature cycles water through the atmosphere to provide fresh water, and the sun cycles its light throughout the world providing energy, nature intended essential life nutrients to also recycle.

Bless you, Ancient Sentinel, for your gifts through growth and death, both essential to earthly life.

The Lord God placed all kinds of beautiful trees and fruit trees in the garden
— Genesis 2:9

The tree stump remembers the climates of the seasons.
— *anonymous*

Decomposition: Nature's Intention

This gap-toothed, black and jagged wooden wall crumbles softly at my gentlest touch. Once erect and sturdy, bowed now and angled askew, it still weaves the divide between forest and meadow. The aged and cracked wall of wood will soon be discarded. Decomposition is the natural environment's recovery plan for nutrients.

As if reading a message transcribed in Braille, my finger traces grooved growth rings still marking its former life, though no living fragrance remains. Seed, soil, sun, and moisture created noble giants, during life's prime reaching 30 feet toward light and cloud. Only those of three-foot diameter and hard-hearted center were selected from the grove, and timbered. Skinned and squared, rough saws chewed ant-high ridge and valley terrain into the living surfaces. Knots, once vibrantly sprouting limbs as large as trunks, now aged into holes, became entrances for grubs, mites, and pregnant female insects seeking nests. Wind, heat, and moisture wearied the wood and extracted living cells, which now lie prone

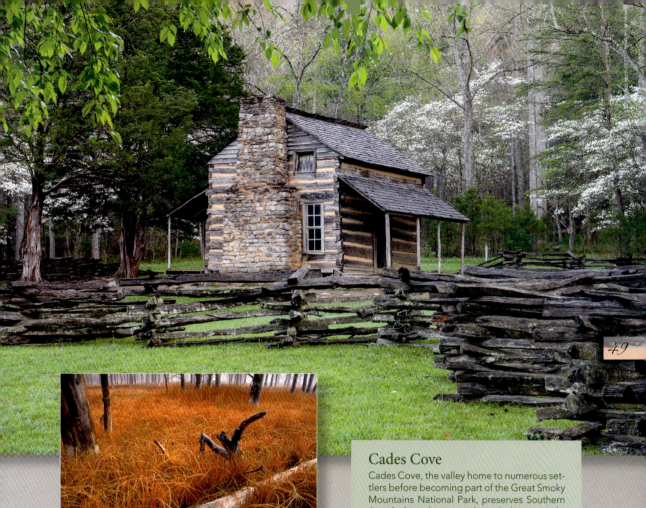

where once they grew upright. Birth decreed decay, nature's recycling.

Human attempts to thwart earth's creation cycle will forever fail. Soaking timbered tree with oil and creosote, itself created from fossil decay, slows only temporarily a loftier architectural plan. Nature accomplishes her design, continually cycling and recycling, rolling creation into death's decay, and through decay, death develops into new creation.

Cades Cove

Cades Cove, the valley home to numerous settlers before becoming part of the Great Smoky Mountains National Park, preserves Southern Appalachian heritage through homesteads, an authentic mill, churches, scenic mountain views and wildlife.

Carloads of visitors driving the 11-mile Cades Cove Loop Road often encounter a "bear-jam" as cars slow for a view of a black bear crossing their path. Listed on the National Register of Historic Places, the road offers 12 distinctive historic features.

Inset: In a burned forest, regrowth begins with grasses.

Above: The original cabin of John and Lurena Oliver, the first permanent European settlers in Cades Cove.

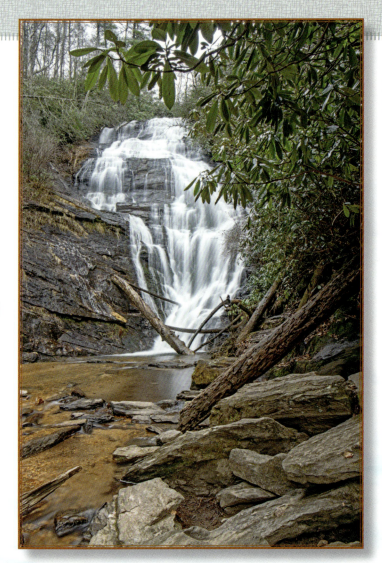

Kings Creek Falls

Blue Ridge *Escarpment*

escarpment — a long steep slope separating two different levels of land

The Eastern Continental Divide follows the mountains from Pennsylvania to Georgia and delineates two watersheds, the Gulf of Mexico and the Atlantic Seaboard.

The Appalachian Mountains run north to south in the eastern United States, but in North Carolina they make a turn to run east-west into Georgia. Some scientists believe that the orientation of this "Blue Wall" of mountains, in combination with prevailing weather patterns and moisture coming out of the Gulf, is a factor in this region having such high rainfall and ecological diversity.

This area of abrupt elevation change between our mountains and piedmont — as much as 2,000 vertical feet! — is referred to as the Blue Ridge Escarpment.

Many magnificent waterfalls result from this drop.

Greenville's unique location, in the South Carolina Piedmont "at the foot" of the Blue Ridge Escarpment, creates diverse habitats. The area boasts more than 150 waterfalls created by this descent, water that provokes vigorous forests of both evergreens and hardwoods, abundant spring wildflowers, gorgeous vistas, unique fern and fungi species, varied wildlife, and many opportunities to escape to calming green and listen for bird songs rather than motors.

Above: Riley Moore Falls

Below: Bull Sluice on the Chattooga River

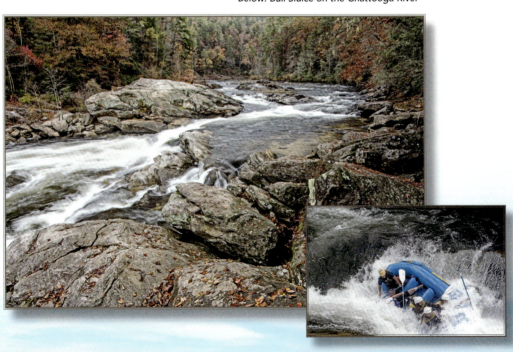

Yellow Branch Falls

Waterfalls

Dynamic geological forces contribute to the creation of waterfalls. Water flowing over rock erodes the softer rock, leaving the bedrock below exposed, and a waterfall results. Earthquakes, volcanoes, and landslides can also cause sudden land alterations.

Waterfall descriptions involve height, width, or average volume of water. Scientists categorize waterfalls based on type of flow.

Enjoy an area excursion and discover various types of waterfalls along our Carolina escarpment!

Waterfalls can be divided into two main types:

Cataract Falls are those with a single vertical drop, usually falling clear of the bedrock. These can be a **plunge** that is taller than it is wide or a **sheet/block**, which is wider than it is tall.

Cascade Falls delineates water descending over an irregular, steep surfaced gradient, usually staying in contact with the river's bedrock. In **rapids**, fast water runs over a less steep bedrock, often involving a series of falls.

Other designations include:

Punchbowl – falling into a wide catch pool, often offering a swim

Plunge – vertical drop without touching bedrock

Multi-step – a series of tiered drops into pools

Horsetail – falls keep contact with bedrock behind it

Fan – falls produce a fan-like shape while contacting bedrock

Chute/Narrows – large volume of water forced through a narrow passage.

Clockwise from top left:
Rainbow Falls in Jones Gap State Park
Spoonauger Falls
Twin Falls, also called Reedy Cove Falls or Eastatoe Falls

Right:
Upper Whitewater Falls, just over the North Carolina line, affirms the Blue Ridge Escarpment.

Below:
Wildcat Falls, also called Wildcat Branch Falls

Issaqueena Falls, at Stumphouse Tunnel Park, is said to be named for an Indian maiden who warned her lover and other white settlers of an impending Indian attack.

The nearby 1,617-foot long Stumphouse Tunnel, an artifact of an 1850s attempt to link the port of Charleston to the cities of the Midwest by rail, provides a glimpse of pre-Civil War engineering.

Wildflowers!

"Nobody sees a flower really;
it is so small.
We haven't time,
and to see takes time —
like to have a friend takes time."

— Georgia O'Keeffe

The Southern Blue Ridge reigns supreme in its diversity of plant species. As the earliest spring sun's warmth creeps into winter's chill, a profusion of wildflowers splash color on the slopes and valleys. Nature photographers, hikers, and wildflower enthusiasts converge on the special places where wildflowers thrive. Some species bloom for only a few days before the hardwood trees begin to develop their new leaves and shade the land below.

A

B

Because each species needs the aid of the other, flowering plants and their pollinators have evolved symbiotic relationships in the natural world.

Birds, bugs, beetles, bees, ants and many other insects perform essential services as they feed; they create continuing generations and a more beautiful world as they pollinate their plant hosts.

Often flowers have developed specialized shapes or structures that work best to attract a certain pollinator.

Bees have a good sense of smell, but do not see red. Thus, bees prefer yellow and blue flowers with dots or lines guiding them to the nectar. Petals provide landing platforms for a pollinator to rest while sipping.

Hummingbirds prefer tubular flowers for their long bill and tongue to reach into and find the desired nectar near the base; they favor red colored flowers.

Night-flying moths obtain their nourishment from flowers that open at night, usually with white blooms and a strong fragrance more easily discovered in the dark.

Butterflies, having good vision but a poor sense of smell, glean during the day from colorful flowers without distinct scents. Because they walk around on the inflorescence, butterflies need flower clusters with landing areas and tubes their tongues will fit into.

An amazing diversity of plant and animal species together create one of this areas' most magical and enticing natural attractions.

A. Pink lady's slipper — *Cypripedium acaule* (April-June)

B. Bloodroot — *Sanguinaria canadensis* (March-April)

C. Showy orchis — *Galearis spectabilis* (April-June)

D. Dimpled trout lily — *Erythronium umbilicatum* (February-April)

E. Carolina lily — *Lilium michauxii* (July-August)

F. Eastern columbine — *Aquilegia canadensis* (March-May)

G. Leatherflower — *Clematis viorna* (May-September)

H. Bee-balm — *Monarda didyma* (July-September)

I. Black-eyed Susan — *Rudbeckia hirta* (May-July)

J. Painted trillium — *Trillium undulatum* (late April-May)

K. Large-flowered bellwort — *Uvularia grandiflora* (April-May)

L. Indian pink — *Spigelia marilandica* (May-June)

M. Wild geranium — *Geranium maculatum* (April-June)

Flowering Trillium

My vote for one of the loveliest flowers opening in the woods in the early spring goes to trillium. Blooming in the light entering the woods before deciduous trees leaf out and covering entire hillsides, this spring ephemeral appears in southeastern woods by the thousands. Hikers time their excursions to known trillium patches to view and photograph this incredible and quickly passing rite of spring.

Around 20 trillium species exist in the Southeast, all in the Lily Family, but divided into two major groups. Toadshade trilliums include those with a stalkless flower attached directly to three mottled and whorled leaves, reminiscent of a frog's or toad's skin.

Wakerobin trilliums bear blossoms on a stalk that arises from three solid green leaves. Three leaves, three petals, and three sepals compose all trillium, thus the name *Trillium*, meaning *three*.

The lovely, delicate flowering follows a convoluted path to its blossom and seed. Usually ants carry the plump, white, oil-rich seeds away from the parent plant, scattering them at the end of the spring blooming cycle, where they will remain dormant until the following spring. Given the right moisture, nourishment, and light, a miniature one-leaf plant

appears the next spring. For six to seven years this tiny plant grows before mature enough to produce a bloom. Finally, if the habitat remains suitable, after many years a single blossom appears, blooming for only a few days.

Trillium flowers emerge in several shades depending on the species and habitat. Some that begin white usually turn pink when pollinated, another trick of nature to enable cross-pollination. A wider variety of insects see the combined color spectrum of white, but this requires more of the plants' energy to produce. Thus, it fades to shades of pink when it completes its work for future seeds.

Various trillium offer distinct odors to attract different insects, another interesting fertilization trick. When viewing the beauty of the blossom, sniff and detect the distinct odors ranging from decayed meat to musty or fruity.

Although once used medicinally, trillium flowers and plants should never be picked. In many states, laws protect them. Plants do not transplant well from the wild. Nursery-propagated plants can be obtained from a growing number of specialty nurseries.

The world was beautiful.... The moon and the stars were beautiful, the brook, the shore, the forest and rock... the flower and butterfly were beautiful.

— Hermann Hesse, *Siddhartha*

Oconee State Park, Oconee Station State Historic Site, and Station Cove Falls

The Oconee Passage section of the **Palmetto Trail** connects these sites. This trail, planned to continue for 425 miles from the South Carolina coast to the mountains, presently crosses much of the South Carolina upstate, most in contiguous sections used for hiking and mountain biking.

The Foothills Trail begins and runs through Oconee State Park.

In early spring the trail to Station Cove Falls offers a profusion of wildflowers including several types of trillium, mayapple, foamflower, hepatica, violets and many other spring ephemerals.

Top: Station Cove Falls; above: Oconee Station State Historic Site includes a 1792 blockhouse from the South Carolina frontier and the 19th century Williams Richards House.

Facing page, middle: Catesby's trillium, rose trillium (Trillium catesbaei); right: Large-flowered trillium (Trillium grandiflorum)

Tulips and Tigers

As it stretches toward light throughout all seasons, an arrow-straight, gray-trunked tulip poplar (*Liriodendron tulipifera*) changes its dress. During winter's chill, erect papery brown pods seem to emerge on every limb, competing with last year's disintegrating triangular fruit bracts.

Camouflaged first by full green leaves, in early spring these pods open into lovely blossoms, lemony green flower cups each marked with an orange swoosh. Stamens dripping yellow pollen vie to fill each cup and stretch above the lip.

Earlier in the yearly cycle the black-striped wings of the sunny yellow eastern tiger swallowtail butterfly, *Papilio glaucus*, fluttered her way to this

Above: Memorable autumn view of Table Rock reflects in Lake Oolenoy at the Table Rock State Park Ranger Station.

Right: Springtime descends at Table Rock Falls on the Table Rock Trail.

tree to lay her eggs as her life waned. Attaching the beginnings of the next generation on what will be their favorite food, she flies off to die.

In spring's warmth, tiny caterpillars emerge, resembling bird droppings to camouflage them from predators, and begin their lifelong munching. As the caterpillars consume their nutrient-laden meals of poplar leaves, they grow too big for their skin. The too tight covering splits and larger caterpillar versions emerge, each turning to eat its former casing. This happens several times until mature enough to attach itself to a tulip poplar leaf and hang in the shape of a "J," awaiting its body's transformation into a papery brown chrysalis.

Waiting patiently again inside this brown mummy wrap, the former caterpillar develops wings that enable flight and a proboscis, a tongue that can unroll into the tulip poplar's nectar-laden blossoms. As an adult butterfly, it sips and grows, continuing this special symbiosis in nature's spiral. Staying close to its source of life-giving nourishment allows the insect to mature into the beautiful butterfly it was meant to be.

The human and the sacred also intertwine to create a symbiotic relationship. If we stay closely connected to the source of our life, the sacred spirit will tend and feed us, making our spiritual natures develop and grow, mature and blossom just as these in the natural world.

Table Rock State Park
Signature of Upstate South Carolina, Table Rock State Park offers recreation, but also quiet nooks with streams and rocks or lakeside trails and cabins. A visitor can find here a most challenging hike or a canoe paddle on a lovely lake, in all seasons.

Caesars Head State Park

North of Greenville near the North Carolina line, on Highway 276, rises Caesars Head, a 3,208-foot high outcrop of granitic gneiss in the Blue Ridge Escarpment.

Caesars Head State Park and Jones Gap State Park connect to form a segment of the Mountain Bridge Wilderness.

The tower area and picnic spots of Caesars Head offer incredible views overlooking the valley below.

Each September the park conducts Hawk Watches during which volunteers count thousands of hawks migrating south using the air currents rising from the lower elevations. This behavior, called *kettling*, saves the hawks' energy for their long migration.

Raven Cliff Falls Trail, its parking lot a little further on 276, offers a lovely moderate hike to exquisite Raven Cliff Falls, the tallest waterfall in South Carolina at 400 feet.

Water Music

Water flowing over rocks in a stream creates some of the sweetest music in nature. The gentle tones bring peace not unlike the quietude of meditation.

Water is the most essential nutrient to life on earth, and the one substance we seek to determine if life resides on other planets. Combining two hydrogen atoms with one oxygen atom (H_2O=water), nature ultimately creates earthly life. Freely provided through the water cycle, we accept this miracle of nature without thought, until we experience either too much or too little.

Many years ago, I heard a story of visitors from the Middle East packing up to leave their extended stay American hotel. When the bellhop arrived to collect luggage, he discovered them in the bathroom attempting to hacksaw off the faucet! Every day in their home region they experienced water scarcity and rationing. This amazing faucet, supplying an unlimited quantity of water just by turning a knob, offered a miracle they did not want to leave without.

All the water draining into a body of water defines a *watershed*, which supplies the water we use. The sun evaporates water; the moisture accumulates in clouds and, when conditions are right, falls to earth as precipitation. Gravity pulls it down the slopes into a body of water at the bottom and into the ground and rocks to be stored as ground water.

If precipitation falls into forested land, the vegetation slows the water, allowing more gradual absorption into the soil, also removing impurities picked up along the water's descent into the watershed. If bare dirt covers the slopes, the moisture flows faster, transporting soil particles and becoming a muddy mixture.

Water falling on vegetated land enters the stream or river, and ultimately the ocean, much cleaner than that which falls on cleared land. Marine life benefits from the cleaner, healthier water, whereas water polluted by sediments can harm life.

Far left: The stately tulip poplar, Liriodendron tulipifera, grows straight and tall throughout Upstate South Carolina.
Left: Thought by some to resemble Caesar's head, the prominent profile gives its name to Caesars Head State Park.
Right: Yellow Branch Falls

In the end we will conserve only what we love,
we will love only what we understand,
and we will understand only what we are taught.
— Baba Dioum, Senegalese conservationist's address

Plants return water and oxygen to the atmosphere through *transpiration*. A grown oak can return 40,000 gallons of water to the atmosphere yearly.

Trees provide summer shade and natural cooling, reducing energy use through less need for air conditioning. A deciduous tree shedding its leaves in winter allows sunlight to penetrate and reduces winter energy use.

Realtors consider that one large tree increases the value of a home by more than $10,000. Retaining vegetation when developing land provides a win-win for humans and the environment.

We drink it, swim in it, boat on it, and play within it; it washes us and everything we use. Protecting water, our essential commons, must be our high priority.

A bridge spans the Middle Saluda River in Jones Gap State Park, a segment of the Mountain Bridge Wilderness.

Jones Gap State Park

connects with Caesars Head State Park and with other preserved land to form the 10,000-acre Mountain Bridge Wilderness. These lands protect and bridge two watersheds and supply Greenville's reputed "best drinking water," Poinsett and Table Rock Reservoirs.

Dogged efforts by environmentally conscientious citizens preserved these state parks and other lands from development. In the 1970s Greenville lawyer Tommy Wyche created one of the first Land Conservation Trusts in South Carolina, Naturaland Trust. Throughout the next four decades, Wyche continued his conservation endeavors to protect the South Carolina Blue Ridge Escarpment. The protection of numerous natural lands and waterways in South Carolina, including Jocassee Gorges and the Chattooga Wild and Scenic River, resulted in large part from his diligence. Naturaland Trust continues the work he began and has spawned much greater environmental awareness in our state. Wyche's books include beautiful photographs and prose that documents his work to retain South Carolina's special places in their natural state.

Delightful trails meander through these parks. Jones Gap receives 90 inches of rainfall a year, thus qualifying it as a temperate rainforest. Its cove hardwood forest miraculously displays a carpet of ephemeral wildflowers each spring and a many-hued leaf-peek each autumn.

This abundance of water forms the headwaters of the Middle Saluda River, South Carolina's first state-designated scenic river, which runs through the park as does the Eastern Continental Divide.

The Middle Saluda River runs through Jones Gap State Park.

Emptiness

Former Poet Laureate of South Carolina James Dickey once discussed the importance of silence in music. Dickey illustrated his concept using Beethoven's Fifth Symphony. He explained that the timed spaces between, along with the notes, together create the immediately recognized sequence and familiar sounds of "ta-ta-ta tum."

Dickey added, "Take lace. The material in lace is not the thing that makes it pretty or catches our eye. It's the space between, the silence, and the emptiness. It's the air that sets the stare," he concluded in his famous poetic fashion, as relayed in a letter by Tom Parks of Midland, Texas.

The space in the lace creates its beauty.

Concert pianist Arthur Schnabel described his talent as one who employs space well. "The notes I handle no better than many pianists. But the pauses between the notes – ah, that is where the art resides," he intones in a *Chicago Daily News* article.

Recent research concludes empty space also enhances brain function. Electronic brain imaging reveals that during silent zoning-out, meditation or contemplation, not thinking about anything specific, our brains work harder than when we concentrate. A specific network of synapses lights up and keeps us consciously aware of ourselves. Science now proves that silence and solitude benefit our growth in self-awareness.

Space. Silence. Emptiness: rare moments in our society. In our living-working-acquiring-doing-enjoying-tossing modern existence, our psyches need to create time when we can push a *pause button* on our world.

But how do we call a cease-fire from life's bombardment?

"Where does a mother go to resign?" perfectly captured my feelings when little ones' needs overwhelmed me. I began my quest to answer this conundrum, discovering where and how I am renewed; I then granted myself permission to find my own *self-space*.

Active experience in nature renews me the most. At times, though, walking away into nature proves impossible, so I created an

Left: Chairs filled with winter snow instead of visitors rest by Rotary Lake, YMCA Camp Greenville.

Below: The Kilgore-Lewis House and Gardens offer serene spots for contemplation.

YMCA Camp Greenville

is owned by the Greenville YMCA and has served boys, girls, and families through several generations.

Located at the apex of the road above Caesars Head, South Carolina, Highway 276, at the state line shared with North Carolina, the naturally exquisite site offers a lake, hiking, meeting venues, and the one-of-a-kind Symmes Chapel, known to locals as Pretty Place.

at-home small retreat area. I added natural objects to recall past excursions: sun-bleached, wave-tossed driftwood that washed onto the sand at my toes; a three-inch emerald pottery vase brimming spruce needles collected on a mountain hike; various colorful, river-smoothed rocks; and a round, brown buckeye for good luck. Pausing alone in this quiet, memory-dominated space, I feel tension release. I regain perspective, renewed.

My family respects my seeking space and honors my retreat. We each discovered that giving the gift of space and silence enhances our lives; we return reinvigorated.

Heritage Preserves

The South Carolina Heritage Trust program began in 1974 and designated the first Heritage Preserve in the United States.

Under the South Carolina Department of Natural Resources, Heritage Preserves conserve natural areas and cultural sites, provide resources for scientific research, and reservoirs of natural and historical elements, as well as habitats for rare and vanishing species.

In South Carolina, 95,000 acres have permanent protection as Heritage Preserves and remain open for public enjoyment during daylight hours.

At Brasstown Creek Heritage Preserve near Sumter National Forest, falls tumble 100 feet in three cascades.

If we perceived Life with reverence,
we would stand in awe at the experience of physical Life
and walk the Earth in a deep sense of gratitude.
– Gary Zukav, The Seat of the Soul

Right: A wooden wagon wheel hewn with rustic tools by work-roughened hands.

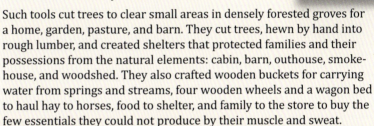

Farm Tools

Rustic tools formed the foundations of southern life a century ago: tools without cords or batteries. Wooden hewn handles sanded smooth as satin by work-roughened hands, powered only by muscled biceps and determined drive, scratched a life from the rock-hard red clay of southern soil.

Such tools cut trees to clear small areas in densely forested groves for a home, garden, pasture, and barn. They cut trees, hewn by hand into rough lumber, and created shelters that protected families and their possessions from the natural elements: cabin, barn, outhouse, smokehouse, and woodshed. They also crafted wooden buckets for carrying water from springs and streams, four wooden wheels and a wagon bed to haul hay to horses, food to shelter, and family to the store to buy the few essentials they could not produce by their muscle and sweat.

Tools opened the ground to grow food for human and animal nourishment. Hand-wielded tools planted, hoed out weeds, and picked cotton. Hands using other tools released the fluffy cotton from its bole, carded the seeds, and then spun it into cotton thread. Plants grown in the garden dyed white cotton thread into colors: yellow from yarrow, blue from indigo, red from bloodroot. These hands then wove the threads into colorful cloth and stitched into clothes, bed linens, and quilts to warm winter nights, while cooking vegetables over a woodstove to feed the family.

They created all essentials for life with their hands employing tools such as these. Incredibly our ancestors' amazing grit, ingenuity, and sweat equity created the foundations of our modern world. What a gift!

Left and below: Two scenes photographed at the Cradle of Forestry in America, Pisgah National Forest.

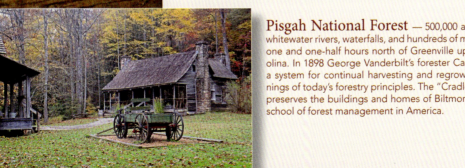

Pisgah National Forest — 500,000 acres of hardwood forest, whitewater rivers, waterfalls, and hundreds of miles of hiking trails — lies one and one-half hours north of Greenville up US 276 into North Carolina. In 1898 George Vanderbilt's forester Carl A. Schenck developed a system for continual harvesting and regrowth of forests, the beginnings of today's forestry principles. The "Cradle of Forestry in America" preserves the buildings and homes of Biltmore Forest School, the first school of forest management in America.

Uncle John's Country Store

A storefront like that of many bygone country stores: chairs await customers and a window reflects the community backbone, the church.

The heavy, faded green door squeaked its welcome, swinging in as I turned the white porcelain knob. Along with the scent of tobacco, pine floors, wooden kegs of nails, and new cloth wound on colorful bolts, we inhaled red clay dust carried on boots stepping straight from plowed cotton fields.

Hearing the "ching-ching" of the cash register signaled my Uncle John's attentiveness to a customer, so my brother, cousins, and I wandered to the back of the store. No matter the hour, a checker game progressed atop the repurposed wooden nail barrel, flanked by twin slat back wooden chairs. We circled around to watch, listening for the tiny thump of black checker crowning red checker and the triumphant scrape of the chair legs against the pine floorboards planed satin-smooth by years of boots shuffled during close games.

When we heard Uncle John's heavy baritone voice wish a customer, "Good Day," our eyes and feet turned toward the long, unpainted pine counter holding the candy jars. Our eager smiles followed his rough hand as he reached into the clear glass for the thumb-sized, creamy-centered chocolate drops, while his other hand shook open a brown paper bag, soon overflowing with this special every-visit treat. Tenderly his rough, king-sized fingers brushed my small, smooth-skinned ones to relay the coveted sack. As he spoke his goodbye, our eyes focused on the prominent Adam's apple bobbing in his tanned and wrinkled neck, like a fishing cork on a windblown lake. "Y'all tell Miss Carrie I'll be 'long soon fur dinner."

Our smiles spoke our thanks as we ran the few blocks to Aunt Carrie's ample bosoms' hug and the welcoming smell of her just-out-of-the-oven homemade biscuits. For us, the blessed nieces and nephews of this childless couple, love was the language communicated throughout this home.

A model of my Uncle John's country store still sits in my playroom 60 years after the excitement and wonder of our childhood visits. Instant messaging, texting, nor Facebook can create a memory equal to this one.

Campbell Covered Bridge

Constructed in 1909 by Charles Irwin Willis, this bridge is named for Alexander Lafayette Campbell, who for many years owned and operated a grist mill at this location. It is the only remaining covered bridge in South Carolina.

Now owned by Greenville County, the passive park includes areas where visitors can picnic, wade in Beaverdam Creek, explore, and learn about the old structures from interpretive signs.

Tender Accountant Hands

"Tender accountant hands," mother laughingly remarked when dad winced passing a hot dish. To me those hands created the visible love that infused my childhood home. Fist strong, but lovingly open, my dad's hands mirrored his life's experience of creating a loving heart from the face of tragedy. It is no wonder that his family's surname is **Love.**

Wordlessly dad's hands recreated the hope and love that anchored his childhood. At our family's home, he expectantly scattered small tan grass seeds on the hard, red clay front yard. Later our family triumphantly admired the lush green growth from his experienced hands, a sharp contrast to his childhood.

At age three, dad lost his mother to tuberculosis, and 18 months later his father died, having caught the 1918 flu while ministering to a neighbor. Orphaned by five, dad's hands clutched the rough sides of the horse-drawn wagon as his dead mother's bachelor brother fetched him and his six-year-old brother to their new home, their grandparents' small, rural South Carolina cotton farm.

Early morning and late afternoon, with walks to and from school sandwiched between, dad's sunburned hands completed farm chores. They guided the old mule behind the plow, planting seeds for rows of cotton, boles spilling soft white fluff for their future clothing. The boys gathered produce from grandmother's garden: corn, okra, tomatoes, potatoes, peppers, and beans. They slopped the pig fattened all summer on garden fodder, then butchered and hung it in the smokehouse for the winter's ham and bacon. They scattered the field corn to plump the chickens. They cut and hauled oak and hickory logs from the adjacent forest that provided winter fires and fuel for cooking. For grandmother's meals those same hands hauled the hand-hewn wooden bucket, water brimming the top, up from the well behind the unpainted clapboard house. They held the tin dipper hung by the well's crank, to cool their

red dust thirst. Only once did my father's hands hold a gun to shoot a squirrel. It was so distasteful an experience he never hunted again.

His strong hands generated beautiful and useful gifts whether grasping hammer, saw, or pencil. As a Certified Public Accountant, he hand-penciled clients' tax returns for 40 years, never requesting an

The original water-powered Hagood Mill

extension. Furniture born from hammer, saw, and used-but-straightened nails transformed our home. Each of his nine children and grandchildren treasure a piece created by his veined and capable hands. Those same hands, tenderly wound around my mother's waist at the kitchen sink, visually communicated the deep love that encircled our home life.

Sometimes those hands also delivered discipline, but I always knew love undergirded the punishment we justly engendered. Once after dinner my sister and I stood at the sink arguing about "who would wash and who would dry." Exhausted by our bickering, dad strode past us and out the door. Cutting a yellow-bell forsythia switch, dad aimed to apply discipline to our legs. As he reentered the kitchen, a small voice near his knees arose from our tow-headed brother. "Dad, I'm on your side!" Dad's blue eyes crinkled at the corners and his stern mouth curved into a smile, the switch in his hands forgotten.

For me those tender hands still live symbolically: openly inviting, encouraging the creation of the extended family's future, lives filled with hope and expressing its name of **Love**.

Hagood Mill Historic Site & Folklife Center

An operating water-powered grist mill built in 1845 by James Pickens, Hagood Mill is listed on the United States National Register of Historic Places.

The property includes two historic cabins, a blacksmith shop, a moonshine still, and a cotton gin. The site also preserves significant Native American petroglyphs.

The property is open Wednesday – Saturday 10-4, and on each third Saturday holds a festival celebrating antique crafts, music, and other activities. A fun family experience!

Above: Canoeing on Lake Oolenoy, Table Rock State Park

Renting a boat or kayak on one of the many quiet lakes surrounding Greenville can be an enjoyable and peaceful activity.

Expanding Circles

The placid water of a secluded cove reflects colorful leaves on its motionless surface. Seeing such quiet water my four-year-old grandson steals away from our nature trail to secure a pebble. He tosses it into the stillness and thrills at the expanding circles he creates.

From a pond bank, I watch enthralled as a bream breaks the surface. It grabs and feasts on a resting iridescent blue dragonfly, each announcing its presence through circles within circles, creating an "ever-widening gyre," as Yeats described in "The Second Coming."

My black lab and I stand spellbound on the dock until the sleek brown otter we spotted realizes he is not alone. Quickly he dives headfirst, disappearing beneath the once motionless surface, leaving only circles on the water to reveal his former presence.

Expanding circles radiate from the center of an impact, energy set into motion. Although gravity keeps us hanging onto our little blue-green planet orbiting around our glowing sun-star, scientists postulate the continual expansion of our universe. Earth's rotation employs the same centrifugal thrust of energy that creates the circles from an impact on water.

Expanding circles of daily life also extend their energy. Positive or negative actions and words create an outspreading circular impact. When I pick up litter on a walk, others see my action and follow, creating a cleaner neighborhood. A student greets a teacher in a friendly manner and this attitude extends to include the class. A doctor demonstrates caring concern for a patient and the patient mentions his appreciation; then new patients call. A resident tells friends about great opportunities in the town and others move in.

In a negative expansion, parents yell when a child interrupts their favorite TV program to share her playdough creation, draining both the relationship and future creativity. A person texting while driving crashes and kills a family on the way to church. Under the influence of alcohol, a college student passes too closely and forces a cyclist off the road, who later dies of head trauma.

Expanding circles of energy released into the world do create an impact, either for good or for harm, a ripple effect that can continue indefinitely just as the once passive pond's circles swell and widen.

> I live my life in widening circles
> that reach out across the world.
> I may not complete this last one
> but I give myself to it.
> I circle around God,
> around the primordial tower.
> I've been circling for thousands of years
> and I still don't know:
> am I a falcon,
> a storm, or a great song?
>
> — Rainer Maria Rilke,
> *Rilke's Book of Hours: Love Poems to God*

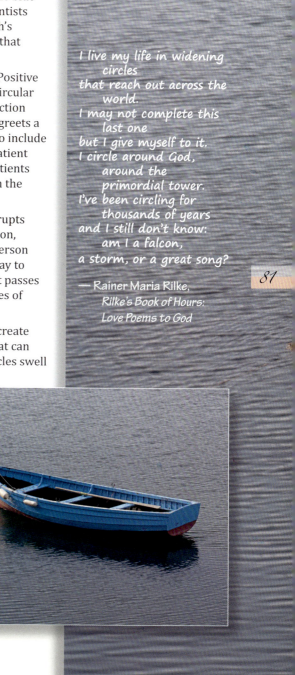

South Carolina Lakes

No natural lakes exist in Upstate South Carolina because no glaciers gouged out holes during the Ice Age. However, numerous lakes created for water, power, and recreation dot the landscape.

Large lakes like Lakes Hartwell, Keowee, and Jocassee flow south together and, along with Saluda, Robinson, Bowen, and hundreds of smaller lakes and ponds, provide fun, fishing, boating, and home sites throughout the Upstate.

Sacred Encounters

A bonfire's haunting glow haloed fellow-campers' faces circled around its flickering flames. Each anticipated this "Last Night Ceremony." Clad in white camp attire silhouetted against the black night, young bodies cast ghostly shadows on bark-covered log seats. With the fire's warmth, our lingering summer songs echoed into the dark forest.

When my turn came, I eagerly stretched my candle into the glowing red embers and watched the wick catch the heat, sparking brilliant orange. I also sensed an additional spark.

A whisper called me to leave the warmth of fire and friendship and venture alone into the dark. I remember the

Many bridges connect sections of the Foothills Trail, which runs between Oconee State Park and Table Rock State Park along the South Carolina/North Carolina state line.

black shadows of the oaks towering over the campfire and the campers' backs huddled toward its warmth as I followed the whisper into the cold dark night, alone.

I did not feel alone in the woods. I felt encompassed by an unseen *Presence*, communion I had never experienced before. I sensed love surround me. In awe, I absorbed the moment completely, forgetting everything else.

Suddenly, I panicked. "What am I doing in the woods alone? I don't want the counselor or campers to be upset by my disappearance."

I fled the woods, leaving the holy *Presence* behind. I returned to my cabin mates.

Back at home the memory of that magical moment in the woods dimmed. I questioned, "Was that real or my imagination? What do I do with this experience? How do I live in two worlds: living intentionally in Holy presence and living to please culture's expectations?"

My identity as a performer and people-pleaser accompanied my birth. I am a second girl who entered life as a scrawny five-pounder with a head full of straight black hair and an adored three-year-old big sister with blonde curls strangers raved over. My mother preserved her father's telegram celebrating my birth: "So happy baby and mother are healthy. Sorry it isn't the boy you hoped for." My parents had one daughter; they wanted a son. I arrived instead.

To cap my family position, when I became the three-year-old big sister, the treasured son arrived, christened as Junior. I became the middle child in this family trio, the spring that flexed between two immovable forces.

As family diplomat, I negotiated through relationship conflicts. Astutely I read personalities and egos, ultimately choosing to do what pleased another. I danced to the drumbeat of others' expectations, not hearing the rhythm of my own heart. In listening for their tunes, my ears dimmed to the call that had pulled me into the camp's forest alone. I left few cracks for holy guidance to squeeze through.

I did follow one admonition: "Take care of the body, for it is a sanctuary." After our kids left for school, I met a friend to hike the meandering forest trails of the nearby mountains, frequently cushioned by pine-needle-quilted carpet. I felt restored returning from a day climbing wooded trails to a mountain's top.

Climbing to those mountaintops, I returned to the lost holy *Presence* I had not acknowledged losing. For me the quiet stillness of the green sanctuary profoundly reveals the sacred.

The Foothills Trail

Woodland beauty surrounds a hiker on the Foothills Trail.

The 77-mile National Recreation Trail traverses the line between South and North Carolina and connects Table Rock State Park with Oconee State Park. It crosses the highest mountain peak in South Carolina, Sassafras Mountain.

Those who hike the entire trail and write about it, receive the Peregrine Award Patch from the Foothills Trail Conservancy. The word Peregrine comes from Spanish "peregrino" meaning pilgrim. The once endangered Peregrine Falcon has also been re-established with nesting sites in the South Carolina mountains that the trail crosses.

Above: Virginia Hawkins Falls on the Foothills Trail

Everybody needs beauty as well as bread, places to play in and pray in, where Nature may heal and give strength to body and soul alike.

— John Muir, *The Yosemite*

Smoky Mountains National Park

A two-to-three-hour drive from Greenville, the Great Smoky Mountains National Park straddles the border between the western edge of North Carolina and the southeastern edge of Tennessee. This most visited park in the National Park system presents additional splendid views and diverse plant and animal life of the Southern Blue Ridge Mountains. Rocky streams and waterfalls dot this UNESCO World Heritage Site and International Biosphere Reserve. Seventy miles of the Appalachian Trail and 850 miles of backcountry trails meander through it.

Thirteen thousand members of the Eastern Band of Cherokee Indians make their home in the Qualla Boundary, which offers the Eastern entrance to the park.

Inset: Roaring Fork Creek in the Smokies

Spread: An observation tower built atop Clingmans Dome, the highest peak, enables unparalleled views of the surrounding mountains and valleys. The park includes 16 peaks over 6,000 feet.

Color Spectrum

Gratefully I live in the southeastern United States with its forests and tree-covered mountains. Folks from treeless regions speak of feeling claustrophobic when visiting where trees dominate the sky. They prefer open spaces with wide unobstructed views.

At dawn, dusk, and after rain I might agree with them. During these transitions in the sun's light, nature offers her most spectacular performances. During these radiant productions, a clear view of the sky can create a visceral reaction for me.

Rainbows, sunrises, sunsets, even blue skies – we witness all colors of nature because our eyes' retinas detect rays of sunlight entering our atmosphere. To our sense of sight this light appears white. But when light passes through a prismatic shaped object, such as a water droplet, the angles within divide the rays of light into the color spectrum.

The white light flowing through a prismatic shape breaks into the ordered rainbow colors of the spectrum. From exterior to interior of the curve the colors merge from red, to orange, yellow, green, blue, indigo, and finally violet. These colors compose the white light our eyes see.

In earth's prism, the white light of heaven breaks into the rainbow colors of life.

It is the same light — unified above, broken open below.

— Joyce Rockwood Hudson,
Natural Spirituality: Recovering the Wisdom Tradition in Christianity

Often following rain, the moisture droplets in the air create this natural light division, and a rainbow results. While driving in arid New Mexico following a light rain, a double rainbow suddenly emerged across the treeless sky. Cars whizzed around us as we stood beside flung-open car doors. My camera captured nature's dazzling display: two multi-colored half circles, one atop the other, arching from horizon to horizon; sunlight colorfully danced through prismatic shaped drops of moisture in the atmosphere.

Each morning the sun's rays of light color the sky. The intensity of the hue depends upon the moisture in the atmosphere. Less moisture intensifies the colors. First various shades of blue emerge because blue rays are the shortest in the spectrum. Sunsets and sunrises reveal the orange and red of light. These longer color rays continue visible to our eyes after the shorter rays disappear from the spectrum.

Ancient people believed that the periods of less intense daylight at sunrise and sunset, the time between light and dark, offered greater opportunity for contact with the spiritual world. These times between times — *liminal* spaces — opened crevices through which the spiritual could more easily enter the earthly realm. The earliest humans considered rainbows a hopeful, graced sign. Rainbows and twilight times viewed with heightened sensitivity offer moments of pure grace.

Blue Ridge Parkway

The Blue Ridge Parkway, known as "America's Favorite Drive," links the Great Smoky Mountains National Park with Shenandoah National Park. It is a linear park running 469 miles along the Blue Ridge Mountains, part of the Appalachian chain. Breathtaking views emerge from almost every mile, and varied length hikes and picnicking spots enhance the drive.

Previous pages: The Linn Cove Viaduct, Milepost 304, opened in 1983 and completed the Blue Ridge Parkway. Built as a concrete segmented bridge to snake around and avoid negative impact to the sensitive Grandfather Mountain environment, it has been designated a National Civil Engineering Landmark.

Double Rainbows

Facing page:
A Great Smoky Mountain sunrise in Cades Cove

*Let me be a living prism,
concentrating the light of love on a transparent world,
a human rainbow revealing grace, peace, and love.*
— *anonymous*

Acknowledgements

Bill and I want to thank the following people for helping us in so many ways.

I am so grateful to my husband, Dr. Harry Shucker, and family members Burgess Shucker, Cherington Shucker, Darin Gehrke, Bonnie and Bill Neely, Jim and Katie Burgess for their continued interest and support throughout. I also want to thank friends Dr. Gil Allen and Martha Severens who agreed to read and offer suggestions on the earliest manuscripts. To Deb Richardson-Moore, thank you so much for the guidance you freely offered throughout this endeavor. I appreciate the careful editing by Lynne Lucas. Thanks also to Steve Marlow, Stephanie Thorn of VisitGreenville.com, my friend Min-Ken Liao, and especially Janie Marlow, who literally took our combined efforts and created such a visually pleasing and informative publication! I appreciate each of you so much!

"Each friend represents a world in us, a world possibly not born until they arrive, and it is only by this meeting that a new world is born." — Anais Nin

— Pam

To Harry Blackwood, my first mentor, who first interested me in the art of photography; to Fran Durovchic, who was first to suggest that a business might be possible; to Steve and Janie Marlow and The Map Shop, who provided and assisted in my first retail sales opportunities; to Ben Keys, who generously shared photography secrets accumulated over a lifetime; to Anne Blythe, my cousin and a successful author, who contributed thoughts and suggestions regarding this book; to Martha Severens, a good friend who also freely gave her professional guidance for the book; to Lynne Scoggins, for her continued support through the years, encouraging me to forge on; and lastly, to Janie Marlow, who has made this book possible with her tireless critiques and suggestions —

To all these encouragers, **Thank you!**

— Bill

Cades Cove

Appendix 1

Selected destinations Round About the Upstate, with corresponding page numbers

Blue Ridge Parkway . . 90
www.blueridgeparkway.org
The Parkway can be accessed via US 25N to I-26N toward Asheville, NC, at I-26 exit #37. Alternatively, via US 276N above Brevard, NC, or via US 178 above Pickens, SC, through Rosman, NC, then NC 215 to the Parkway.

Campbell Covered Bridge 77
www.greenvillerec.org/campbellcoveredbridge
171 Campbell Covered Bridge Rd, Landrum, SC 29356

Cades Cove 49
in Great Smoky Mountains National Park

Chattooga National Wild and Scenic River. 51
Chattooga Conservancy
www.chattoogariver.org
Portions of the movie "Deliverance" were shot on the Chattooga, which forms the northwestern border of SC.

Cleveland Park 16
www.greenvillesc.gov/clevelandpark
Cleveland Park Dr & East Washington St, Greenville, SC 29601, *also accessed along McDaniel Ave*

Cradle of Forestry in America 75
www.cradleofforestry.com
11250 Pisgah Hwy,
Pisgah Forest, NC 28768
828-877-3130

DuPont State Recreational Forest . . 46
www.dupontstaterecreationalforest.com
Visitor Center
89 Buck Forest Rd,
Cedar Mountain, NC 28718
828-877-6527

Foothills Trail 85
www.foothillstrail.org
The Foothills Trail begins at Oconee State Park and terminates at Table Rock State Park. It can be accessed from either park and at numerous intermediate sites.

Furman University . . . 32
3300 Poinsett Hwy,
Greenville, SC 29613
864-294-2000

Gorges State Park . . . 43
976 Grassy Ridge Rd,
Sapphire, NC 28774
828-966-9099

Great Smoky Mountains National Park 86
Over 520,000 acres and 800 square miles divided equally between NC and TN. Oconaluftee (1194 Newfound Gap Rd, Cherokee, NC 28719) is the nearest Visitor Center to Greenville. Sugarlands (1420 Little River Rd. Gatlinburg, TN 37738) is another. 865-436-1200

Jocassee Gorges
(*officially the "Jim Timmerman Natural Resources Area at Jocassee Gorges"*). 43
www.dnr.sc.gov/managed-wild-jocassee
In 1998 Jim Timmerman along with John E. Frampton, two leaders in the South Carolina Department of Natural Resources (SCDNR), worked with many businesses and conservation groups to protect this largest parcel of contiguous mountain property ever protected from development, 35,000 acres in SC and 17,000 in NC.
The SC Visitor's Center is located at Keowee-Toxaway State Park, 108 Residence Drive, off Cherokee Foothills National Scenic Byway (intersection of SC 11 and SC 133), Sunset, SC 29685. 864-868-2605.

Kilgore-Lewis House and Gardens. 26
www.kilgore-lewis.org
560 N Academy St,
Greenville, SC 29601
864-232-3020

Lake Conestee Nature Park 25
www.lakeconesteenaturepark.com
840 Mauldin Rd,
Greenville, SC 29605
864-277-2004

McKinney Chapel. . . . 35
Cleo Chapman Rd,
Sunset, SC 29685
Located within the Cliffs Keowee Vineyards Community; tell the gate attendant your destination.

Palmetto Trail. 61
Palmetto Conservation Foundation
www.palmettoconservation.org
803-771-0870

Pisgah National Forest Ranger Station 75
https://www.fs.usda.gov/nfsnc
1600 Pisgah Hwy,
Pisgah Forest, NC 28768
828-877-3265

Pretty Place 19
Symmes Chapel (*locally known as "Pretty Place"*) YMCA Camp Greenville

Prisma Health Swamp Rabbit Trail . . 28
https://greenvillerec.com/prisma-health-swamp-rabbit-trail
864-288-6470

Rock Quarry Gardens . 22
www.greenvillesc.gov
then *Search*.
200 McDaniel Ave,
Greenville, SC 29601
864-467-4350

SC Botanical Gardens . 37
150 Discovery Lane,
Clemson, SC 29634
864-656-3405

Springwood Cemetery 35
410 N Main St,
Greenville, SC 29601
864-467-4324

Stumphouse Tunnel Park
& Issaqueena Falls . . . 55
Stumphouse Tunnel Rd,
Mountain Rest, SC 29664

Sumter National Forest's
Andrew Pickens Ranger
District
*consists of 85,000 acres
in Oconee County.*
www.fs.usda.gov/scnfs
Office location:
112 Andrew Pickens Cir,
Mountain Rest, SC 29664
864-638-9568

World of Energy 43
Oconee Nuclear Station
www.worldofenergy.com
7812 Rochester Hwy,
Seneca, SC 29672
864-873-4600

YMCA Camp
Greenville 71
www.ymcacamp
   greenville.org
4399 YMCA Camp Rd,
Cleveland, SC 29635
864-836-3291

Selected Area Waterfalls

*For a list of and directions to 100 SC waterfalls see
www.upcountrysc.com/explore/waterfalls/*

Brasstown Creek Falls 72
US 76, Westminster, SC
29693

Bull Sluice 51
*On the Chattooga River
at US 76 bridge*

Chau Ram Falls
Chau Ram County Park
1220 Chau Ram Park Rd,
Westminster, SC 29693

Falls Creek Falls
Jones Gap State Park

Issaqueena Falls 55
Stumphouse Tunnel Park,
SC Hwy 28,
Walhalla, SC 29691

Kings Creek Falls 50
Burrells Ford Rd,
Mountain Rest, SC 29664
*Kings Creek is a tributary
of the Chattooga River,
on a spur of the Foothills
Trail.*

Laurel Fork Falls
on the Foothills Trail

Rainbow Falls 53
Jones Gap State Park

Raven Cliff Falls 64
Caesars Head State Park

Reedy River Falls 11,12,13
Falls Park on the Reedy,
601 S Main St,
Greenville, SC 29601

Riley Moore Falls 51
Sumter National Forest,
Andrew Pickens Ranger
District
Spy Rock Rd &
Forest Service Rd 748C,
Westminster, SC 29693

Rock Quarry Falls 22
McDaniel Ave,
Cleveland Park,
Greenville, SC 29601

Spoonauger Falls 53
Burrells Ford Rd,
Mountain Rest, SC 29664
*Spoonauger Falls is
on a tributary of the
Chattooga River, near
Burrells Ford.*

Station Cove Falls . . . 61
Sumter National Forest,
Andrew Pickens Ranger
District
500 Oconee Station Rd,
Walhalla, SC 29691

Table Rock Falls 63
Table Rock State Park,
Table Rock Trail

Twin Falls/ Reedy Cove
Falls/ Eastatoe Falls . . 53
152 Waterfalls Rd,
Sunset, SC 29685

Upper
Whitewater Falls 54
*Drive north on SC 130,
which becomes NC 281.
Falls is on the right just
over the state line.*

Virginia Hawkins
Falls 85
on the Foothills Trail

Wildcat Branch Falls/
Wildcat Falls 54
Wildcat Wayside State
Park, 5325 Geer Hwy
(US 276), Cleveland, SC
29635

Yellow Branch Falls .52,65
Sumter National Forest,
Andrew Pickens Ranger
District, 3023 SC 28 S,
Walhalla, SC 29691

Selected Preserves, Heritage Preserves (HP), and Historic Sites in Upstate South Carolina

Ashmore HP
45 Persimmon Ridge Rd,
Cleveland, SC 29635

Bald Rock HP
Geer Hwy (US 276)
(4.6 miles south of
Caesars Head State Park),
Cleveland, SC 29635

Blue Wall Preserve
off Pennell Rd near Tryon,
NC, and Landrum, SC.
See directions at
https://www.nature.org/
en-us/get-involved/
how-to-help/
places-we-protect/
blue-wall-preserve/

Brasstown Creek HP . 72
Forest Service Rd 751,
Long Creek, SC 29658

Bunched Arrowhead HP
150 McCauley Rd,
Travelers Rest, SC 29690

Buzzards Roost HP
Buzzards Roost Rd,
Walhalla, SC 29691
864-868-0281

Chestnut Ridge HP
Oak Grove Rd,
Landrum, SC 29356

Eastatoe Creek HP
US 178N above Hwy 11,
turn left at sign for Laurel
Valley Lodge. *Park in
Foothills Trail parking lot
and follow signs.*
Sunset, SC 29685

Eva Russell Chandler HP
Persimmon Ridge Rd,
Cleveland, SC 29635

Glassy Mountain HP
662 S Glassy Mountain
Church Rd,
Pickens, SC 29671

**Hagood Mill Historic Site
& Folklife Center** 79
www.visitpickenscounty.com
138 Hagood Mill Rd,
Pickens, SC 29671
864-898-2936

**Musgrove Mill
State Historic Site**
398 State Park Rd,
Clinton, SC 29325

Nine Times Preserve
Trailhead parking at
approximately 1550,
1750, and 2000 E.
Preston McDaniel Rd,
Sunset, SC.
https://www.nature.org/
en-us/get-involved/
how-to-help/
places-we-protect/
nine-times-preserve/

**Oconee Station
State Historic Site** . . . 61
Oconee Station Rd,
Walhalla, SC 29691

Pacolet River HP
445 Lucky Lane,
Spartanburg, SC 29302

Peter's Creek HP
www.spartanburg
conservation.org/
properties/peters-
creek-heritage-trust-
preserve
556 Kelly Rd,
Spartanburg, SC 29307

Poinsett Bridge HP . . . 38
580 Callahan Mountain Rd,
Travelers Rest, SC 29690

**Stumphouse Mountain
Heritage Preserve** . . . 55
Stumphouse Tunnel Rd,
Mountain Rest, SC 29664

State Parks (SP) in Upstate South Carolina

Caesars Head SP 64
8155 Geer Hwy (US 276),
Cleveland, SC 29635

Croft SP
450 Croft State Park Rd,
Spartanburg, SC 29302

Devils Fork SP 43
161 Holcombe Rd (off
Cherokee Foothills
National Scenic Byway
(SC11), Salem, SC 29676

Jones Gap SP 68
303 Jones Gap Rd,
Marietta, SC 29661

Keowee-Toxaway SP . 44
108 Residence Dr, off
Cherokee Foothills
National Scenic Byway
(SC 11), Sunset, SC 29685

Kings Mountain SP
1277 Park Rd, Blacksburg,
SC 29702

Lake Hartwell SP
19138 Cherokee Foothills
National Scenic Byway
(SC 11), Fair Play, SC
29643

Oconee SP 61
624 State Park Rd,
Mountain Rest, SC 29664

Paris Mountain SP . . . 33
2401 State Park Rd,
Greenville, SC 29609

Sadlers Creek SP
940 Sadlers Creek Rd,
Anderson, SC 29626

Table Rock SP 63
158 Ellison Lane, off
Cherokee Foothills
National Scenic Byway
(SC 11), Pickens, SC
29671

Wildcat Wayside SP . . 54
5325 Geer Hwy (US 276),
Cleveland, SC 29635

Appendix 2

Alphabetical list of photographs, with page numbers

Blue boat on lake 81

Caesars Head 64
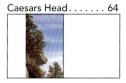

Double rainbow 90

Furman University . 31,32

Blue Ridge Parkway &
Linn Cove Viaduct . 88-89

Campbell
Covered Bridge 77

DuPont State
Recreational Forest,
Lake Julia 46-47

Gardens at Falls Park
on the Reedy 14

Burned forest 49

Cleveland Park creek . 16
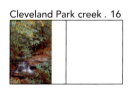

Ferns. 36

Great Smoky Mountains
National Park 86-87

Cades Cove . . . 48,49,92

Country store 76

Foothills Trail 82,85

Cradle of Forestry
in America 74-75
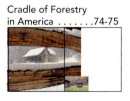

Hagood Mill Historic Site
& Folklife Center . .78-79

Jones Gap State Park . .66-67,68-69

Lake Keowee 44

Poinsett Bridge 39

Spider web. 28-29

Liberty Bridge 14-15

Reedy River Falls . .12-13

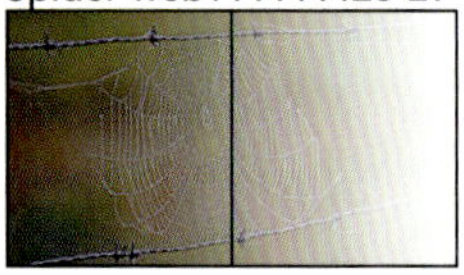

Springwood Cemetery 35

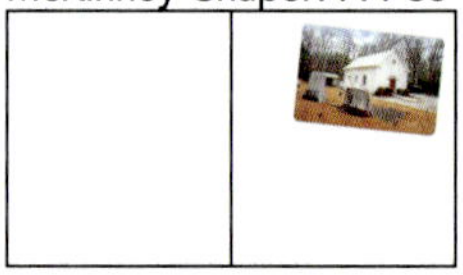

Kilgore-Lewis House and Gardens. 26, 71

McKinney Chapel. . . . 35

Rock Quarry Gardens & Falls 20-21,22

Table Rock State Park, Lake Oolenoy. 62,80

Oak near Caesars Head. 6

Lake Jocassee . 40-41,42

Sunflower 35

Tree at sunrise 91

Oconee Station State Historic Site . . . 61

Sunflower and bee 23,24

Tulip poplar flower. . . 63

Paris Mountain State Park. 33

Waterfalls
. 50-55,61,63,65,72-73,85

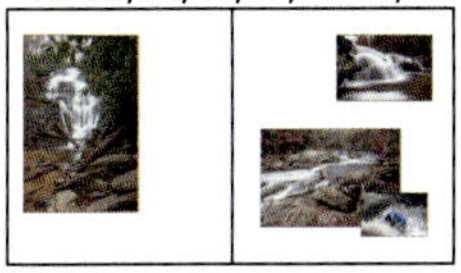

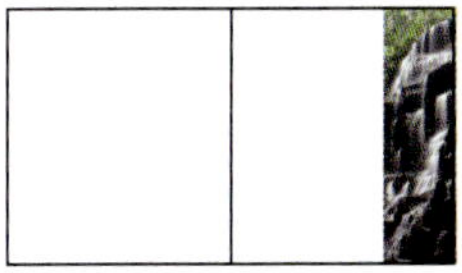

Wildflowers
. . . . 2,43,56-59,60

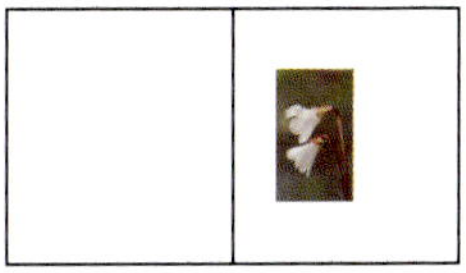

Wooden hand-hewn
wagon wheel 75

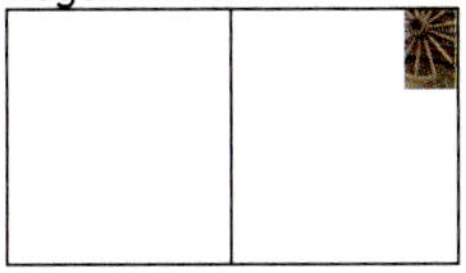

YMCA Camp Greenville,
Symmes Chapel
("Pretty Place"),
Rotary Lake 19,70

Window reflection . . . 78

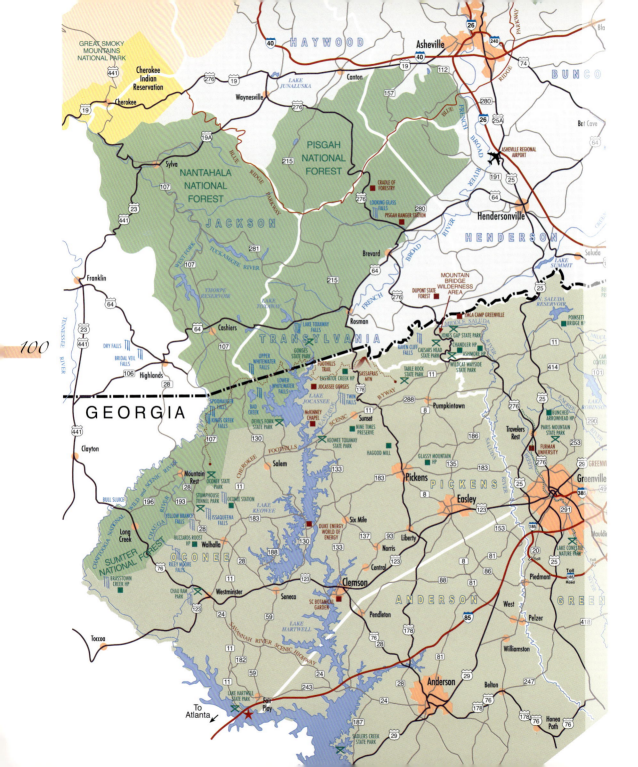

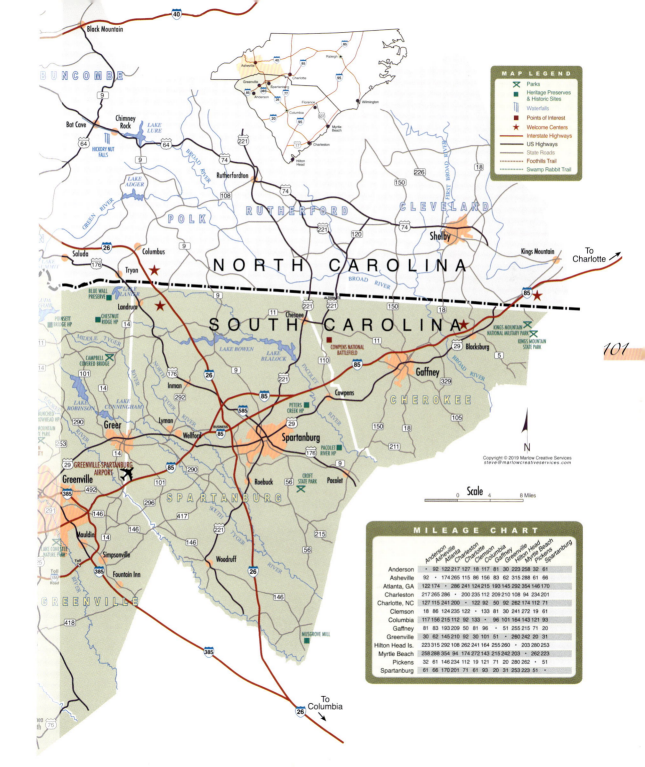